Jerry has blessed us all with a marv
book is God-glorifying, Bible-cente
read by any person who desires loving himself/herself and others as well as
to be loved.

Simon Tsoi, Executive Director
Chinese Baptist Fellowship of the U.S. and Canada

I am pleased that Dr. Corbaley's writing follows his speaking style; that is,
he presents some of his most insightful thoughts with a "twinkle in his
word processor". I encourage all who desire a deeper walk with the Lord
Jesus Christ to read and reflect on *The Most Excellent Way*.

Lonnie Wascom, Director of Missions and Ministries
North Shore (Louisiana) Baptist Associations

Jerry's book has challenged me at the deepest level. This is a book that
needs to be taken in small bites and then allowed plenty of time to digest. I
commend it to any believer serious about knowing and loving God.

Sam Morgan, Pastor
New Hope Baptist Church, Creswell, OR

In these times of turbulence, disagreements, and conflicts, Jerry Corbaley's
The Most Excellent Way reminds us that we will be measured by nothing
more or less than the love that we live in and live out each day. Written
with passion, urgency, and poetry Corbaley's book brings us back to the
greatest of the spiritual gifts and compels us, in light of this most excellent
way, to redefine our sense of who we are.

David Garrison, Author, *Church Planting Movements*
Regional Leader for South Asia, International Mission Board, SBC

This generation seeks for the truth apart from the love of God. Thus this
book helps us to find the truth in relationship to the Great Commandment
of our Lord Jesus in His Holy Word that we are to implement in every area
of life.

Paul Kim, Baptist Convention of New England President
Founding Pastor, Berkland Baptist Church, Cambridge, MA

Jerry Corbaley's book, *The Most Excellent Way*, is an excellent biblical-based devotional book that will help one focus on pleasing God. May the Lord use this book to be a blessing to the Body of Christ.

Rochelle Davis, Jr., Pastor
Temple of Faith Baptist Church, Detroit, MI

The Most Excellent Way lives up to its title. It challenges the reader to focus intentionally on the love of God and on loving God's way. This focus, taken to heart, has the power to transform our churches, our families, our relationships, and our lives.

Wes Kenney, Pastor
Trinity Baptist Church, Valliant, OK

If success in life depends on keeping the main thing as the main thing, then Jerry Corbaley's book makes a real contribution. As God a millennium ago used St. Bernard's book on the four levels of love to launch an awakening in France, may He bless your reading of this book toward a new millennium of obedience to the New Commandment.

Rick Durst, Professor of Historical Theology
Golden Gate Baptist Theological Seminary

The Most Excellent Way is a needed addition to Christian maturity and spiritual-growth literature and will be of special interest to any woman desiring to be more influential in others' lives. The author's discussion of the Great Commandment is thought-provoking and challenging. This is indeed a book to give to someone who wants to be like Jesus.

Linda M. Clark, Women's Specialist
California Southern Baptist Convention

Without any reservation, I encourage you to read carefully this book and to allow the love of God to become your catalyst and motivation in the on-purpose returning of His love toward Him and toward others.

Charles E. Smith, Jr., Global Evangelist
President, Charles Smith Ministries Sturgis, MS

Jerry Corbaley's book, *The Most Excellent Way*, returns us to the Master's focus in discipleship. By recovering the centrality of love in the Christian faith, Corbaley brings a much-needed correction to what is often marketed as "biblical Christianity" by the churches in America. Corbaley's work has strengthened my walk with Christ. I trust the same will be true for you.

Paul H. Chitwood, Kentucky Baptist Convention President
Senior Pastor, First Baptist Church, Mt. Washington, KY

We live in times in which people have many questions about life issues. The book gives the reader hope, answers, and a place to start to confront life's challenges based solely on the Word of God and with the love of God.

Michael A. Gonzales, Hispanic Initiative Director
Southern Baptists of Texas Convention

I found *The Most Excellent Way* very interesting and informative. I so appreciate Jerry Corbaley's approach and interpretation of the Great Commandment. This is a book that all Christians need to read.

Bill Sanderson, Pastor, Hephzibah Baptist Church, Wendell, NC
Carolina Conservative Baptist Convention President

If you think, as I did, that you know something about the love of God, <u>read this book!</u> It will change your entire concept of God's love versus human love. Jerry Corbaley's writing is revolutionary yet most biblical. This book is a <u>must</u> for your Christian library.

Bobbie Horton Caldwell
Sunday School Teacher (40 years), Temple Baptist Church, Simpsonville, SC

Reading *The Most Excellent Way* made me desire to apply the Great Commandment and the New Commandment in every area of my relationships and especially to my Lord. Paul's statement that *The love of Christ compels us* (2 Cor. 5:14) takes on a new reality after reading this book.

John Floyd, Administrative Vice President, Mid-America Bapt. Theological Seminary
Chairman, Board of Trustees, International Mission Board; Emeritus Missionary

The Most Excellent Way is a gold mine of insight and wisdom where key elements of living and practicing the Christian life are concerned. Every Christian and seeker-after-God can find something helpful and applicable.

C. Preston North, Pastor
Mountain View Baptist Church, Lake Isabella, CA

Printed in the United States of America
by Lightning Source, Inc., LaVergne, TN
Cover design by Dennis Davidson

All Scripture quotations, unless otherwise indicated, from the
Holy Bible, *New International Version*, copyright 1973, 1978,
1984 by International Bible Society.
Library of Congress Control Number: 2006931617
ISBN 0-929292-44-8

Hannibal Books
P.O. Box 461592
Garland, Texas 75046
1-800-747-0738
www.hannibalbooks.com

TO ORDER ADDITIONAL COPIES, SEE PAGE 224

The
MOST EXCELLENT
Way

An Intentional Focus on
God's Greatest Priority

JERRY CORBALEY

Dedicated
to

those who desire to be like Jesus Christ in this world.

If you have any encouragement from being united with Christ, if any comfort from his love, if any fellowship with the Spirit, if any tenderness and compassion, then make my joy complete by being like-minded, having the same love, being one in spirit and purpose (Phil. 2:1, 2).

Same love, one spirit, one purpose.

Contents

Foreword

I consider myself a Jerry Corbaley fan. We met because we both are trustees of the International Mission Board. In these marathon meetings that take place at least every two months, you can get to know someone well. How the person thinks and feels is revealed because the pressure of reaching the world brings out the deepest passions of a person and spreads them out for others to examine and consider.

I am a fan because Jerry, on many occasions, has given us the deeper perspective on critical issues. His logic is Bible-based; his conclusions and his ability to articulate them are more than intriguing.

As you read this book, you will grow to appreciate what we on the board know about Jerry Corbaley. He is a godly man with a gift for finding and sharing God's heart. Because of that you will find this book a great read. More than once or twice your eyebrows will be raised because of his unique approach. Soon you will be drawn into the work as a life-application study.

The subject most written about in both sacred and secular history, the most explored emotion within the human experience, and the most misunderstood word in history all are titled *love*.

In Jerry Corbaley's *The Most Excellent Way* you will discover both the full definitions and extensive applications of this subject. This work is meant to provoke life change in you and in your church.

As I read the book, I found that I could not simply read through it. I discovered that I found times when I had to put the book down and think and research and pray and think again. Challenges to my ability to love and receive love were made not just by the author. I found that as truth was laid upon truth, I was entering new ground in at least my application of this well-storied matter called *love*.

That word *application* is the one principle missing in much of what we heretofore have read about this subject. How do we really do this act called *love*? Can we really love as God loved us? Do I really love and can I judge myself in this matter? All of these questions will be answered in these next pages.

My prayer is that the Lord will use this book to stir an awakening in your life and in the lives of our churches. Such a change within us will fix everything that is missing around us in causes such as evangelism and missions. Join my friend, Jerry Corbaley, on a journey deep into the love of God. May the Great Commandment become the great passion of your life.

Thomas Hatley, Pastor
Emmanuel Baptist Church
Rogers, AR
Chairman, 2004-2006
Board of Trustees, International Mission Board

Preface

Our Creator gives spiritual insight. We depend on Him for the ability to understand anything from His point of view. This book is for those who have totally surrendered their own wills to the Lord Jesus Christ. Until you have done so, this book never can be more than an interesting point of view that points out the hypocrisy of individual Christians. To the humble, it is much more than that.

The Infinite Creator is all-wise, eternal, all-powerful, and everywhere. By definition He is infinitely aware of every detail about each of us. You have an infinite amount of His attention. While we can be awestruck by the beauty and intricate complexity of this world, we seldom reflect that this world is a foul shadow of what it once was. The curse of sin has been at work for more than 6,000 years.

Evil truly is in the world. A truly infinite and loving Creator does exist. The best questions to ask are, "What does He expect of me? How do I please Him?" Others may prefer the philosophical approaches that do not result in a desire to know Him. Let each one do what he or she wants.

I find the Bible to be a supernatural message. I believe it is as accurate as if God spoke the words Himself. I have found nothing else to compare with the accuracy of the Bible in explaining "me" to me. I find nothing else remotely relevant in defining the world in which I live.

This Bible reveals that the Creator God became a person in Jesus Christ. He was sent to dwell among the people of His own creation to demonstrate how we are to live. That is what this book is about. Now that we have eternal life through Christ, what does it look like?

He also was sent to pay our penalty for sin. God reveals Himself to be holy and just. His justice requires eternal punishment for the offense of even one sin. For this to be just, sin must be infinitely worse than you or I can imagine. Sin must be so terrible that an eternity of conscious torment cannot atone for it. Some may choose to concentrate on the philosophical questions without application. But do you have the practical humility to believe that the Infinite God can know how bad sin is, even though your finite self cannot? Without beginning at this point of humility, you stand no chance of pleasing His divinity.

Before I was old enough even to understand the concept of sin, I had many sinful habits. I never had a chance to be sinless. I rejoiced at my chance to be forgiven.

Jesus' sinless life and eventual death on the cross literally paid an infinite penalty of torment, because a perfect and infinite being was tormented. Infinite torment literally was paid in full. Jesus Christ is God himself. All humankind now may approach the Holy and Infinite God without the terrible condition of sin preventing us from doing so.

God actually will draw some of you to Himself through the following Scriptures.

"No one can come to me unless the Father who sent me draws him, and I will raise him up at the last day. It is written in the Prophets: 'They will all be taught by God.' Everyone who listens to the Father and learns from him comes to me" (John 6:44, 45).

Jesus answered, "I am the way and the truth and the life. No one comes to the Father except through me. If you really knew me, you would know my Father as well" (John 14:6, 7a).

13

*That if you confess with your mouth, "Jesus is Lord,"
and believe in your heart that God raised him from the
dead, you will be saved. For it is with your heart that
you believe and are justified, and it is with your mouth
that you confess and are saved* (Rom. 10:9, 10).

Will you do so? Will you respond to your Creator? If you
will humble yourself and change your attitude toward Jesus
(repent), then He will change you and give you the desire to
live a holy life (also repentance). Joy and fulfillment will
become a consistent and repetitive reward. He will receive you
as His own child if you care enough to submit to Him.

Will you surrender your will to Him? He did make you. He
will do what He wants to do with you. Will you trust Him?
Begin your awareness of His presence by talking to Him. This
is what prayer is—talking to a very real God. For your part,
begin the relationship by asking Him to forgive you of your
sin. Thank Him for paying your penalty of torment on the
cross. Talk to Him as if He rose from the dead and rules the
universe, because He did and He does. Ask Him to change you
into whatever He wants you to be. You will not be disappointed. You will be astounded at how real He is and how much He
cares for you.

If you just made such a decision and just had such a con-
versation; then would you tell me so at *corbaley.blogspot.com*?
I would like to celebrate with you. Jesus Christ is our Savior,
Lord, and eternal companion. He is more real than I am.

For those of you who already are Christians, do not stop
doing the ministry that you prefer. The message of this book is
for every language group. It is for every culture. This book is
not about a new "paradigm". This book reveals how you may
be most effective in your paradigm of choice. If you are mis-
sional in outlook, lovingly do so. If you are purpose-driven in

outreach, lovingly be so. If you prefer the Sunday School model of church, lovingly continue. God neither is upset nor impressed with your cultural preferences. He will empower them all, but He will do so His way. He has a Great Commandment.

I have never done anything perfectly in my life. That includes this book. Every time I review it, I find something I would like to change. I convince myself they are "improvements". You may not agree. If you set me straight, I will appreciate it. Your suggestions for improvement are preferred to mere criticism.

I would like to thank everyone who encouraged me during my life. I have too many to list everyone. But I would especially like to thank Lynn, my bride of 29 years, who has nurtured me through decades of trial and error and error and error. Sweetheart, no human will cheer louder or longer than I will on the day your faithfulness is rewarded. You are one of my heroes. I love you in every way imaginable. To the readers: If you are going to marry someone who is smarter than you are, make sure the person is Christian.

I also wish to thank and encourage my four children, Wes and Sarah (Corbaley) Childers and Chris and Stephanie (Grady) Corbaley. All four of you are more mature in Christ than your mom and I were at your age. God is blessing you all. That blessing will continue as long as you treasure it. We have no greater joy than to know that our children are walking in the Truth.

I wish to thank all of those who were willing to endorse this book. I deeply appreciate your kind words and the risk of your own good names. When I read what you had to say, I was frequently surprised and embarrassed too seldom. For your sakes I hope you know what you are talking about.

I also thank Southern Baptists as a whole. You are not the only fishing boat on the lake, but you are known as real fishermen. Jesus is building His church throughout the world. His grace has made you fruitful. Since 1977 you have nurtured me and have no one to blame for me but yourselves. May God bless us with another faithful generation.

The integrity of this message stands on the integrity of the life of Jesus Christ. He is your perfect example. The lines of reason within this book rest on the Bible, the Word of God. May God have mercy on me if I have twisted His message. The success of this book as a change-agent in your life rests on your faith. Believe what you want. Just be sure you purposely do so.

Have the courage to think the thoughts.

I do love you.

Jerry Corbaley
Deep in the Redwood Rainforest of California
September 2006

Chapter 1

What Does Jesus Most Want Us to Do?

One of them, an expert in the law, tested him with this question: "Teacher, which is the greatest commandment in the Law?" Jesus replied: 'Love the Lord your God with all your heart and with all your soul and with all your mind.' This is the first and greatest commandment. And the second is like it: 'Love your neighbor as yourself.' All the Law and the Prophets hang on these two commandments (Matt. 22:35-40).

Overemphasizing the importance of the Great Commandment is virtually impossible. Nothing is more important. Love is the most excellent way. It is God's first priority. To love God with all your heart and with all your soul and with all your mind will take all your time. All the Law and the Prophets hang on the priorities of these words of Jesus Christ. Love actually fulfills the Law. Everything depends on the love of God.

In the Bible God has given us His very words. They are inerrant. They are true concerning moral values, historical narratives, and miracles. The writings of the apostles and prophets are as if God Himself breathed them.

Not only has God told us what is right and wrong, true and false, He also has made plain the fact that some truth is more important than is other truth. Priorities of what is right exist. Certainly the Ten Commandments reflect moral priority over the distance between the metal pomegranates in the tabernacle.

Certainly the truth that salvation is found in no one other than Jesus Christ is more important than is the least of the spiritual gifts. Certainly removing the speck from our brother's eye is important, but not until we have removed the beam from our own eye.

Above all other true priorities is the Great Commandment. Once you are born again, the Great Commandment is the unifying truth from which all other priorities descend. Your obedience to God's great priority will affect the amount of blessing you receive from Him. Your obedience to God's great priority is God's ultimate goal about the discipline you receive from Him. Supposing that the Creator does not notice, nor remember, who takes his Great Commandment seriously is absurd.

Consider this illustration. It is a composite of many of the things Jesus has told us.

God who became a person called out to the people of the world, "I am the way, and the truth and the life; no one comes to the Father but through Me. I will pay the infinite penalty for your sin, personally and literally, through My blood shed on the cross. I will rise from the dead. All power and authority has been given to Me. I will make you a new creation—a very child of God. I will live within you by My Spirit; you will thrive with eternal life. I will build My church and will accomplish exactly what I want to do in the world. I am the infinite God. I will be Savior to those who humble themselves and treat Me as their Lord.

"You must become My disciple. You must take My yoke upon you and cooperate with me. I have a great commitment to loving you; you must have a great commitment to loving Me and all humanity, as I define love. To love God and all humanity My way is My absolute priority. You must obey My Great Commandment. You must bear much fruit. You must glorify Me, My way. As you are going, make disciples of all nations. I will hold you accountable. You have no excuses. My burden is easy; My yoke is light. As you have faith in Me, you cannot fail. At the end, perfection and paradise will be yours, forever".

Multitudes responded to the call of God, Who became a person. As the decades and centuries passed, many different groups emphasized many different priorities of the Master. Some groups emphasized, above all, the calling to the harvest.

With great zeal these servants entered into their calling. They pulled the weeds. They watered the grapes. They drove off thieves and varmints. They pruned the vines, polished the grapes, repaired the stakes, and swept the barns. They sang praises to the Master. They encouraged each other with the Master's words. They would die for the grapes; some of these servants actually did. They diversified into harvesting different kinds of grapes. They harvested great, heaping piles of grapes. They assumed that great, heaping piles of grapes was the best way to please and glorify their Master.

Yet on the day of accounting their Master was not pleased with most of them. He called them wicked and worthless servants. He said they were annoying nobodies who would gain nothing from the Master's hand. He said that He did "not even know them".

They were upset. They reminded the Master of all their labor and sacrifice and good work. So the Master asked them if they had loved God and all humanity and done it the Master's way. He reminded them they were to bear much fruit as well as to harvest grapes. They had to admit that they didn't know the Master was so serious about actually loving Him and all people. Besides, they could not agree on what "loving" was.

To those who barely entered into their Master's happiness, He said, "At least you loved me and all humankind indirectly, on occasion, though incidentally. Now understand clearly; I am love. The expression of love is what glorifies Me. Now grow up and live, on purpose, the life of love, with all of your heart, all of your soul, all of your mind, and all of your strength, as I promised you from the day I gave you eternal life."

This illustration is not an exaggeration. Ignoring the Great Commandment is absurd. Having memorized the Great Commandment is not enough. Zealously doing many good and important things is not enough. The "end" does not justify the "means". Indeed, the love of God is more than merely a "means" to an "end". The love of God is both the "means" and the "end". To obey the Great Commandment, we actually must obey the Great Commandment.

From the next passage consider how important love is:

"If I speak in the tongues of men and of angels, but have not love, I am only a resounding gong or a clanging cymbal. If I have the gift of prophecy and can fathom all mysteries and all knowledge, and if I have a faith that can move mountains, but have not love, I am

nothing. If I give all I possess to the poor and surrender my body to the flames, but have not love, I gain nothing" (1 Cor. 13:1-3).

This passage speaks of a resounding gong and a clanging cymbal. Neither can be endured for long. After a period of time the gong and cymbal become unendurable. They become annoying. No matter what language we speak, if we do not express ourselves in love, the situation becomes annoying.

The second sentence speaks of prophecy, fathoming mysteries, knowledge, and a faith that can move mountains. All of these are spiritual values that involve thinking. No matter what you think, if you do not have love, you are nothing.

The last sentence of the passage speaks of actions—what you do. Whether you give all your possessions to the poor or whether you die a martyr's death by being burned at the stake—if you have not love, you gain nothing.

Consider the following accurate synopsis of this same passage.

No matter what I say, without love I am annoying. No matter what I think, without love I am nothing. No matter what I do, without love I gain nothing.

We can reduce this even further and still contain the essential truth.

Without love I am an annoying nobody who gains nothing.

Again consider this synopsis. Are you at peace with this interpretation? Do you have a better one? Throughout the book again and again I will repeat it.

This Corinthian passage covers my words, my thoughts, and my actions. That covers pretty much all I am and all my time. Without love I am an annoying nobody who gains nothing. Compare this thought with 1 Corinthians 13:8a: "Love never fails". That is quite a contrast.

The illustration of the master and the servants just presented is accurate! As we apply it to ourselves, two questions emerge. First, do I know what *love* is? Second, am I loving God?

Here is what God says *love* is:

> *Love is patient, love is kind. It does not envy, it does not boast, it is not proud. It is not rude, it is not self-seeking, it is not easily angered, it keeps no record of wrongs. Love does not delight in evil, but rejoices with the truth. It always protects, always trusts, always hopes, always perseveres. Love never fails*
> *(1 Cor. 13:4-8a).*

Take a moment and reflect on your Christian pilgrimage up to this point. Have you chosen to focus your attention on loving God this way? Have you committed His definition of *love* to memory so that you, on purpose, can do it and avoid confusion and indecision? When you measure your moral values alongside God's definition of *love*, does the harmony of the two encourage you? Do you spend any time comparing your moral values to God's expressed priority? Is the Great Commandment the defining purpose of your life? When you notice that you are not loving, do you confess it as sin so that you will be forgiven and purified?

Since overemphasizing the importance of the Great Commandment is virtually impossible, being sure we are on the right track is vitally important.

Do I treat God lovingly? Since love is patient, am I patient with Him? Since love is kind, when I talk to Him in prayer, am I kind to Him? Since love does not envy (therefore love is content), do I want what He says I can't have? Do I brag to Him about how good I am? Do I prefer my opinions to His? And so on down the list. He has been very clear about what He says *love* is. In all your words, love God. In all your thinking, love God. In all your actions, love God. To treat God this way fulfills the Great Commandment. All other truth descends from this priority. When you, on purpose, love God, you are obeying the Great Commandment. All the blessings of God flow toward you without restriction.

When you love God, you are fulfilling the law. Consider:

"You shall have no other gods before me" (Ex. 20:3).

Isn't putting a false god before the real God unkind and rude toward God? Isn't doing so prideful and self-seeking? Isn't idolatry delighting in evil? Compare the previous three questions to what God, in 1 Corinthians 13, says *love* is. You will see that if you are loving toward God, you are fulfilling the Law, because love is kind; it isn't rude, proud, nor self-seeking. Love does not delight in evil but rejoices in the truth.

Bible-believing people will not be surprised to know that the books of the Bible are mutually supporting and mutually enlightening. Jesus told us that the Scripture cannot be broken.

Comparing the rest of the Ten Commandments with the definition of God's love will reveal that loving God fulfills the Law.

"You shall not make for yourself an idol. You shall not bow down to them or worship them . . ." (Ex. 20:4-5).

Isn't making an idol unkind and rude toward the real God? Isn't doing so prideful, self-seeking, and delighting in evil? If your passion is to love God with all of your heart and all your soul and all your mind, you do not want to make an idol nor worship it. You will be fulfilling the Law.

"You shall not misuse the name of the Lord your God" (Ex. 20:7).

Remembering how you reacted when people have misused your name is not difficult! To use the name of God lovingly is your birthright as a Christian. When your first priority in life is the Great Commandment, you do not want to misuse the name of God. You are fulfilling the Law.

The Law, the Prophets, and the Apostles represent the content of the Bible. While we often may have been driven to our knees before God because of despair and guilt, the Bible is filled with promises of blessing that give us hope. We hope for the blessings of God. We can look at these in two ways— blessings of grace and blessings that are a reward for obedience. (These are not absolute divisions; a significant overlap exists.)

The blessings of grace are not earned. God gives them to us because of who He is. He chooses to bless for His own reasons.

The blessings that we receive as rewards, however, are directly related to our faithfulness to obey what God has said. And we have a Great Commandment. A decision on your part to, on purpose, love God with all your heart and all your soul and all your mind will enable God to bless you accordingly.

Don't be surprised that such a commitment on your part will result in a new awareness of virtually everything in the Bible. Since the Great Commandment fulfills all the Law and the Prophets, consider how Old Testament patriarchs, judges, prophets, and kings related to God. Did God bless them in relation to their loving Him? Absolutely. Jesus did not wait until the time of Matthew to "invent" the Great Commandment. He quoted it from the book of Deuteronomy:

> *"Love the Lord your God with all your heart and with all your soul and with all your strength. These commandments that I give you today are to be upon your hearts. Impress them on your children"* (Deut. 6:5-7a).

Notice that we are to impress them on our children. So, of course, you have impressed on your children the absolute priority of the Great Commandment. After John 3:16, we want them to memorize the Great Commandment and the definition 1 Corinthians 13:4-7 gives of the love of God. A wonderful goal for parents is to enable their children to reach adulthood with health, education, and the virtue of knowing and habitually practicing the love of God. The most important thing for a Christian parent to impress on his or her children is the love of God. We succeed in this only when we have done it ourselves by, before them, setting a living example.

Look again at what God says *love* is. Ask yourself whether these qualities describe your spontaneous desires. Do you, on purpose, act and react this way without choosing to do so?

> *Love is patient, love is kind. It does not envy, it does not boast, it is not proud. It is not rude, it is not self-seeking, it is not easily angered, it keeps no record of wrongs. Love does not delight in evil, but rejoices with the truth. It always protects, always trusts, always hopes, always perseveres. Love never fails* (1 Cor. 13:4-8a).

25

We, on purpose, can love God only when we know what love is and when we, on purpose, choose to love. When your love of God becomes habitual, we can call it virtue. When we are not loving God, we can call it sin and repent of it. If you will do this, then He will purify you. The blessings that He promises will begin to flow without restriction to you. You will enjoy all the blessings of grace and all the blessings of obedience. Surely the rewards for obedience are not expendable nor contemptible!

> *If we confess our sins, he is faithful and just and will forgive us our sins and purify us from all unrighteousness. If we claim we have not sinned, we make him out to be a liar and his word has no place in our lives* (1 John 1:9, 10).

If for decades we have lived as Christians and have not, on purpose, chosen to love God with all our hearts and all our souls and all our minds, then we are rather like the multitudes harvesting the vineyard. These multitudes never bothered to find out what *love* meant. Perhaps we have not realized how seriously the Master takes His Great Commandment. This tragic sin results in little blessing and stunted spiritual growth. Perhaps His words are not remembered and treasured, because "his word has no place in our lives" (1 John 1:10). How many years can we live unloving lives, never calling what we do *sin*, until He concludes we are making Him out to be a liar? God will take that personally. According to this Scripture, His Word then will have no place in our lives. Decide for yourself: Does a relationship exist between those who do not memorize Scripture and those who do not know what God says *love* is? Can I justify my "inability" to memorize what my Lord has said is most important by asserting that I cannot memorize

Scripture? The inability to memorize Scripture actually is just an excuse for refusing to memorize Scripture. Does a refusal to admit sin remove God's Word from having a place in our lives?

The Great Commandment is an absolute priority. You can kill varmints for Christ and polish grapes until you die, but doing so will not please your Creator. You may, indirectly, occasionally, and incidentally, obey the Great Commandment as you stack up great, heaping piles of grapes. But that is not faithfulness with all your heart and all your soul and all your mind. Either you choose, on purpose, to obey the Great Commandment, or you choose to please Him indirectly, occasionally, and incidentally, if at all. Habitual, conscious effort will lead to habits of virtue. Soon you will be doing by habitual reflex what you once considered impossible. As you mature, you will attain to the whole measure of the fullness of Christ. This is a goal worthy of your greatest priority and therefore your greatest effort.

Now, this is not difficult. It is a matter of believing what Jesus has said and then, on purpose, trying to do it. Since the Great Commandment is the first priority of God, He always will give grace and strength to those who want to obey the Great Commandment. This is God's expressed will for you. When you cooperate with Him about what He considers to be most important, you can count on His most direct participation in your life. He rewards faithfulness. He wants to work shoulder-to-shoulder with you.

> *"Come to me, all you who are weary and burdened, and I will give you rest. Take my yoke upon you and learn from me, for I am gentle and humble in heart, and you will find rest for your souls. For my yoke is easy and my burden is light"* (Matt. 11:28-30).

Is your yoke easy? Is your burden light? Learn from Jesus. Find rest for your soul. Working with Him is easy; what He wants you to carry is light. If this does not describe your Christianity, consider starting with the Great Commandment.

Hurry—time for us to move on to the New Commandment!

Chapter 2

We Have a New Commandment

Don't you find interesting the fact that Jesus did not allow the lawyer to frame the answer He wanted to give?

One of them, an expert in the law, tested him with this question: "Teacher, which is the greatest commandment in the Law?" Jesus replied, "'Love the Lord your God with all your heart and with all your soul and with all your mind.' This is the first and greatest commandment. And the second is like it: 'Love your neighbor as yourself.' All the Law and the Prophets hang on these two commandments (Matt. 22:35-40).

When asked about the greatest commandment, Jesus included a second commandment that was like it: *"Love your neighbor as yourself."* Then He declared that all the Law and the Prophets hang on these two commandments. Our Master considers these two commandments to be alike. Both are more than the Law and the Prophets combined. Indeed the two commandments are so much alike that our faithfulness to one is equivalent, in His mind, to our faithfulness to the other.

If anyone says, "I love God," yet hates his brother, he is a liar. For anyone who does not love his brother, whom he has seen, cannot love God, whom he has not seen. And he has given us this command: Whoever loves God must also love his brother (1 John 4:20-21).

(See also Matt. 25:40, 45)

This relationship seems to be very clear. If I do not love my brother, I am not loving God. If my brother is not loving me, then he is not loving God. The results of such behavior in my spiritual life and in my human relationships are the same as if I (or my brother) were sinning. That is because we are sinning if we are not loving each other God's way. We are not doing what God wants done. We are not faithful to His Great Commandment. We are not fulfilling the Law.

But loving God and our neighbor fulfills the Law. In the last chapter we looked at how loving God literally fulfilled the first three of the Ten Commandments. Let's not take as much time here, but the rest of the Ten Commandments literally are fulfilled by loving your neighbor as yourself. If you are loving your neighbor God's way, you do not bear false witness nor murder nor commit adultery, nor do you covet. Love does no harm to its neighbor; therefore love is the fulfillment of the Law.

We forever will be grateful that our Savior, Jesus Christ, paid our debt on the cross, so we don't suffer eternally. Yet with God, sin remains a serious issue. He wants us to remember that sin—often without remedy—can rip all of our earthly relationships to shreds.

Remember the synopsis of 1 Corinthians 13:1-3?

> No matter what I say, what I think, nor what I do, if I am not loving, I am an annoying nobody who gains nothing.

If breaking one of the Ten Commandments is sin, and all the Law hangs on the commands to love God and your neighbor, then refusing to follow the Great Commandment and the

New Commandment is sin. Loving God and your neighbor fulfills the Law. Refusing to do so breaks the Law. The biblical word for annoying nobodies who gain nothing is *sinner*. Our heavenly Father has better things in store for His children. Hopefully His children want them.

Jesus has termed the instruction to "Love your neighbor as yourself" a new command.

> *"A new command I give you: Love one another. As I have loved you, so you must love one another. By this will all men know that you are my disciples, if you love one another"* (John 13:34, 35).

What are the implications of the New Commandment? The on-purpose loving of each other is the essence of discipleship. Those who claim to be disciples of Jesus Christ are found to be loving each other God's way. This is how we know who is of God. This is how we know what religion is true and what denomination is true and what church is inhabited by Jesus Christ.

If our faithfulness to God is defined by our conscious commitment to love God with all our hearts and all our souls and all our minds, and the relationship between the Great Commandment and the New Commandment is equivalent, then loving our neighbors with all our hearts and all our souls and all our minds defines our faithfulness.

Let us again consider God's definition of *love*:

> *Love is patient, love is kind. It does not envy, it does not boast, it is not proud. It is not rude, it is not self-seeking, it is not easily angered, it keeps no record of wrongs. Love does not delight in evil but rejoices with the truth. It always protects, always trusts, always*

hopes, always perseveres. Love never fails
(1 Cor. 13:4-8a).

Recognize that the love of God is not based on emotion. While people who love "God's way" will get emotionally involved with the truth (love rejoices with the truth), and while emotion and the love of God may affect each other, recognizing that the love of God is a chosen behavior, regardless of how you "feel" about it, is of primary importance.
We cannot afford to miss this point.

Love, as defined by God, is a chosen behavior. We choose, on purpose, to love. Sometimes my emotions carry me on a wave of euphoria in which I "feel" like being patient, kind, unselfish, and full of hope. But God wants me to be patient, kind, unselfish, and hopeful whether I "feel" like it or not. That is why the Bible never says "Thou shalt 'feel' like obeying the Lord thy God." Obedience is a necessary virtue of the New Covenant as well as of the Old Covenant. Overcoming our feelings with our minds is what separates us from animals. Animals use their minds only to execute what they feel. Overcoming our feelings with our minds is what God has created us to do.

We cannot afford to miss this point.

Love, as defined by God, is a chosen behavior. While emotions are God-created and He wills that we experience them in our lives, remember that He places a superior emphasis on our believing what He has said. Also remember that emotions are affected by sin and are not trustworthy, no matter how sincere. They are, by definition, sub-rational. But faithfulness is rational. Faithfulness is doing, on purpose, what God has said to do. In fact, the word *emotion* does not appear, as such, either in the Old or New Testaments. The Biblical synonyms for this God-intended experience would be *passion* and *sensuality*. When your passions and sensuality are guided by the Great Commandment and the New Commandment, then you are living a holy life as God intends. Enjoy the life He has given you, but enjoy it His way (Why destroy yourself?). As you become mature in on-purpose loving, you (with His help) will harmonize your emotions with the will of God so that your emotions will motivate you and bring you joy in a holy manner. The Holy Spirit will make sure that your emotions fulfill their intended purpose.

Love as defined by God is a chosen behavior. Once you are willing to believe this, then you have a blessing in store. You will realize that, with practice, love becomes a skill. And skills may be improved. Skills may be practiced. Skills may be used at will. You can become as good at loving God and your neighbor as you want to be. The Holy Spirit always will empower you to do what God wants done. He wants you to become very, very good at it. The Holy Spirit's great priority is the same as are the priorities of God the Father and God the Son. Love God and your neighbor God's way. In doing so, you can be as blessed as He wants you to be. To the extent that you, on purpose, love others, you will accomplish the will of God. Love never fails. Love fulfills the Law. Acting on purpose to love God's way always accomplishes the will of God. You will be a blessing.

Let's go back to the New Commandment. What difference does it make in my life? If it makes a difference, my life will be characterized by patience with God and with others. To be patient with my brother or sister is to be patient with my heavenly Father. You make a huge mistake if you miss His emphasis on this. Our lives will be characterized by kindness, contentment, modesty, humility, politeness, and unselfishness. We shall be known as ones who can hold our temper, forgive others, rejoice with the truth, build trust, protect others, and persevere under hardship while we maintain hope. We shall be known as those who never fail God. You can do what God says is most important. You can love Him with all your heart and all your soul and all your mind and your neighbor as yourself.

Christians who love God's way are known as the salt of the earth and the light of the world. Say, now! You actually know how to be the salt of the earth and the light of the world! Such people will be like Jesus. So we're not surprised when God says:

"All men will know that you are my disciples if you love one another" (John 13:35).

This is, of course, how you determine if you are on the right track in your pilgrimage toward heaven. Are you, on purpose, cooperating with the Great Commandment and the New Commandment? Does your commitment include loving God and your neighbor with all your heart and all your soul and all your mind? Does this affect all of your time?

As you spend months and years developing your skill at on-purpose loving, you will gain wisdom as to how to love people most effectively. For example: in your workplace, when someone is angry, do you first apply kindness or try to protect the person from hurting himself or herself or others? Do you have time to use politeness to soothe the rough edges? Or do you have to risk your physical health to confront the angry person and unselfishly make yourself the target for his or her emotional venting? After the angry episode is over, do you know how to build trust? Will admitting your own faults help? Are you content to work with the person God has placed before you? Do you know how? Why not become good at it? Do you have something better to do?

Love is a skill. On purpose, do it! Be blessed. Be a blessing. At work, how many people do you know who, on purpose, love others God's way? Why not become one of those people? Notice that those who, on purpose, love others never are bored. They never are lonely. They never are "down" for long. They always are willing to admit their own sins, though their sins usually are "minor" compared to everyone else's. They are the ones who are welcome in lives that are having difficulty. They are the ones who listen. They are the ones who succeed. They are the ones who are more interested in doing God's will than in getting recognition for their "godliness". Their joy is in serving others by loving them God's way. Doing this is their treasure—their purpose for all eternity.

Love is a skill. Skills are developed by practice over time. Training is practice over time. When times are good, practice loving the ones who are easy to love. As God says, train yourself to be godly. Get good at this, because the time will arrive when you are called on to love the "unlovable".

> *"But I tell you: Love your enemies and pray for those who persecute you, that you may be sons of your Father in heaven. He causes his sun to rise on the evil and the good, and sends rain on the righteous and the unrighteous. If you love those who love you, what*

reward will you get? Are not even the tax collectors doing that? And if you greet only your brothers, what are you doing more than others? Do not even pagans do that? Be perfect, therefore, as your heavenly Father is perfect" (Matt. 5:44-48).

And so we get down to another testing of our faith. Can you love your enemies in the way God loves His enemies? He causes the sun to rise on them and sends the rain to bless them. We all are on this earth to experience and weigh the knowledge of good and evil (Gen. 2:9b). Both the righteous and the wicked still have good and evil entering their lives. We won't escape it until this world kills us or until Jesus returns. God causes some blessing to enter the life of everyone, because God loves even His enemies. Everyone on the planet and throughout history also has experienced patience and kindness from God. He is not easily angered toward the wicked. He is willing to forgive the unrighteous if they will repent through Jesus Christ. God has loved the world. He doesn't command us to do what He will not do Himself. He continually sets the example for us. We are to love our enemies as He loved us when we were His enemies.

Once you realize that love is a chosen behavior, you can, on purpose, love people even if you emotionally don't like them. Isn't that amazing? You can be patient with someone who is impatient with you. You can choose to be kind and polite with those who are unkind and rude toward you. You can try to build trust with those who currently are untrustworthy.

With experience and wisdom you can recognize when you need just to persevere in someone's presence instead of leading that person to rejoice in the truth. Everything has its time.

A prudent man sees danger and takes refuge, but the simple keep going and suffer for it (Prov. 22:3).

If making peace with your enemy is possible, then loving that person God's way is the way to succeed. If you are patient, kind, content, modest, humble, polite, unselfish, and hold your temper, then you will have few enemies. They will have to be directly and purposefully antichrist to hate you! If you are loving them with the love of God and they are treating you as though you are their enemy, then God is the One they hate, isn't He? Can you imagine how twisted someone must be to return your love with sin? What an adventure when God sends you to untwist the person!

When a man's ways are pleasing to the Lord, he makes *even his enemies live at peace with him (Prov. 16:7).*

Even if you hate my guts but love me God's way, and you are good at doing this from years of maturity, you will treat me better than if you loved me emotionally but occasionally were (and sincerely) selfish, rude, mean, angry, hurtful, and delighting in evil. Much of the time, having a mature Christian for an enemy is more pleasant than is having a non-Christian for a friend.

Let's look again at the New Commandment passage.

"A new commandment I give you: Love one another. As I have loved you, so you must love one another. All men will know that you are my disciples if you love one another" (John 13:34, 35).

Shining the light of Scripture on ourselves first always is most important. We need to know that we are pleasing our

Savior. Since this is His will for us, we can know that He will enable us to love each other. But recognizing who loves and who does not also is important.

The scope of this book does not include addressing whether an unloving person in the church actually is a lost person or is a wolf in sheep's clothing. Just as likely as not, the unloving person simply is an infantile Christian who thinks that being born again is the be-all and end-all of Christianity in this world. Likely this person does not know any better. Likely this person is following the best examples he or she has found. Likely the best examples he or she has found treat Jesus as "Lord" in an indirect, occasional, and incidental manner. Likely we are living in the last days in which:

> "*Because of the increase of wickedness, the love of most will grow cold*" (Matt. 24:12).

Regardless of how much power the unloving have accumulated in a church or how much honor they receive, they are not the examples for Christians to follow. Rather, those who are faithful to love God with all their hearts and all their souls and all their minds and who love their neighbors and their enemies are the ones to follow. These are the only ones filled with the Holy Spirit.

Just reading these passages is not the same as is living these passages. Rejoicing in this truth is not the same as is living this truth through years and decades to become mature. Remember that criticizing is easier than is leading. Doubting is easier than is succeeding. When I am frustrated and ready to give up on those around me, this happens because I do not know what to do about the problems either!

Knowledge puffs up, but love builds up (1 Cor. 8:1b).
Love never fails (1 Cor. 13:8a).

As you observe nonsense among last-days "Christianity", remember to pray that God's people will be loving. If we do not have because we do not ask, and other last-days Christians do not have because they do not ask, then none of us is loving God's way, because none of us is asking for the love of God. Why not start asking? Pray that God's people will be loving. Pray that they will be wise. Pray that they will be faithful. As the Apostle Paul prays for us:

And this is my prayer: that your love may abound more and more in knowledge and depth of insight, so that you may be able to discern what is best and may be pure and blameless until the day of Christ, filled with the fruit of righteousness that comes through faith in Christ—to the glory and praise of God (Phil. 1:9-11).

Chapter 3

We Have Cultural Pollution

What an interesting time in which we live! When a person tells me he or she is a worshiper of Jesus Christ, I have found that asking which Jesus the person worships is important. False christs and false prophets abound. Life is very interesting.

Across the nation and across denominational lines I have been taking an informal poll. To those who claim to worship Jesus Christ, I ask several questions. I am not out to embarrass nor to offend anyone. I just want to know if my perception is correct. As American Christians, what do we know about which we seek? (Incidentally, my definition of *Christian* is more stringent than is that of most Evangelicals).

When I ask Christians what the Great Commandment is, I get accurate answers about 80 percent of the time.

When I ask what the New Commandment is, I get accurate answers about 25 percent of the time. When I ask if we are to love each other, I get accurate answers about 98 percent of the time.

When I ask people what *love* is, I get an accurate answer about five percent of the time. Almost everyone knows about 1 Corinthians 13, but 95 percent of Christians have not committed it to memory.

So for these reasons (and several others) I have concluded the following:

We know about the Great Commandment but little about the New Commandment.

We are not aware of the relationship between loving God and loving others. Therefore, we are lax in applying the Great Commandment.

We know *where* to find out what *love* is, but we seldom bother to remember *what love* is.

We rarely even consider that the love of God is something that we, on purpose, choose; therefore, we are content to be passive, as if God is supposed to make us "feel" love toward Him and others. Since we do not believe we, on purpose, love, we do not, on purpose, try.

We do have a high regard for Scripture. As a consequence, we often love indirectly, occasionally, and incidentally. We indeed are blessed by grace. But our lack of focus costs us the many rewards that spring from mature faithfulness. While we love God, people, and even our enemies indirectly, occasionally, and incidentally, doing this does not yield the same blessings as does on-purpose loving.

Loving God and others with all your heart and all your soul and all your mind is not attained by immature sincerity, nor is it attained by time and chance. No matter what I say or think or do, if I have not love, I am an annoying nobody who gains nothing.

Across the land, Christian people do not know what the *love of God* is. But they think they do. Everyone has an opinion about what *love* is. However, the blessings and disciplines of God do not hinge on your opinion but on God's opinion. He is right because He is God and He is infinite. He does not subject the definition of *love* to the scholar, the actor, the artist, nor to majority opinion. He is not impressed with the depth of our sincerity.

Across the land, Christian people have a polluted understanding of the love of God, because several different types of "love" have us confused. Each of these types of polluted love clearly can be seen and understood.

These polluted loves are so persuasive for two reasons. One is that virtually all your friends and neighbors sometimes call them "love". The other reason is that these polluted loves all are real. All people experience all of them. The "pollution" does not spring from a lack of reality but from the mistaken (sinful) conclusion that God defines His love in the way Americans define *love*. Let's look at these "loves" that pollute Christian understanding.

Infatuation as love

Infatuation is an unreasoning passion — an irrational attraction. Infatuated people are deprived of sound judgment; their intellectual powers are weakened. Synonyms of infatuation include *folly, madness, intoxication, foolishness,* and *unreason.* Infatuation certainly is real, but if left alone it is not healthy. Infatuation is sub-rational.

When a child falls head-over-heels in "love" with another child, this is infatuation. Certainly you can remember what this was like. You cannot think about anyone but "her". You do not eat. When you finally sleep, you dream of "her". All of your life is dominated by an emotional attraction to "her". You are not reasonable. You are not rational. You are obsessed. You don't want to be rescued.

As we get older, infatuation remains our companion. We are irrationally attracted to expensive cars, grandiose careers, houses, fame, wealth, and power. The temptation to acquire is magnified by the fact that infatuation is so much fun. It truly is enjoyable. It always is enjoyable. It is one of the most intense of all human joys. Infatuation is overpowering. The problem is that infatuation is irrational and never lasts. Never.

I always have regretted long-term decisions that I made because I was infatuated. When I am carried along by a multi-day/-week/-month emotional high, I am unaware that it is temporary. My body will not sustain the euphoria caused when my blood is saturated with molecules released by infatuation. Just because it is a natural, God-created high does not mean it cannot be addicting and sub-rational. The addiction to emotional infatuation is every bit as damaging as is addiction to any mood-altering drug.

Love at first sight is infatuation. No care is given to whether moral values are compatible. No exploration of moral values is attempted. The two people have "fallen in love". It feels so right that it cannot be wrong. The consequences of his or her past are unimportant and unexplored. "My love will change him (her)", the person reasons. When the infatuation evaporates, the person falls "out of love". When a person has decided that love and infatuation are the same thing, the person has locked himself or herself into a sub-rational lifetime of chasing infatuation and leaving a string of discarded loves behind.

Infatuation is real. We all experience it. We may be infatuated with a new job or a new house or a new pastor. It is just as real as are earth and sky. And it is enjoyable. New Christians even are infatuated with their new lives in Christ. Nothing in human experience compares with being born again unless it is dying or experiencing the physical return of Christ to earth. Infatuation is real and enjoyable, but it is sub-rational and temporary. Infatuation is not the love of God.

Let's run infatuation by some of the things God has said.

"By this will all men know you are my disciples, if you are infatuated with one another". Hmmm. I don't think that works.

"But I tell you, be infatuated with your enemies." No, no. That doesn't work, either.

Infatuation is real, but it is not the love of God. As Christians, be crystal clear on this. When God talks about the Great Commandment and the New Commandment, He is not talking about infatuation.

Romance as love

Romantic love is real, but it is a cultural phenomenon. Our cultures have molded us to expect certain behaviors and characteristics regarding falling in love and living happily ever after. It sounds like a fairy tale or a fable because it is. Saint Valentine neither is prophet nor apostle and probably is highly offended by what Americans do in his name.

Romance in my culture is rooted in the chivalric behavior of the Middle Ages of Europe. The knight rescuing the damsel in distress. The quest to earn a woman's favor. The heroic act that saves the kingdom and earns the princess' admiration. The giving of exorbitant gifts. Even sacrificing your life in battle to defend your loved ones.

In our time romantic love expresses itself in similar, though more tame, ways. We give a gift of fur from a once-vicious chinchilla. We storm the gate (to the yard) to retrieve a sweetheart from her parents. To prove our courage we even may fight the barfly. This is a little nuts, but it is real. The whole culture plays by a set of rules. Now, when the rules are not sin, then going along is worth doing. The cultural ideal is a little nuts, but everyone believes it is real. So if you do not go along, they will conclude that you are the one who is a little nuts; that is of no advantage to you. Pick your battles. Buy some flowers for your wife.

Unfortunately, such a thing as romantic infatuation exists. This is where the slightly nutty cultural ideal of falling in love and living happily ever after meets the emotional obsession that is sub-rational. This immediately can be dangerous. This is the point at which jealously turns to rage, anger turns to murder, and courtship turns to stalking.

However, for our purposes, comparing romantic love to some of the passages we previously have examined is enough. "You shall be romantically involved with God with all your heart and all your soul and all your mind." Well, actually, that isn't terribly bad. Just don't, for Christ, beat up drunks, okay?

Let's try another. "By this will all men know that you are my disciples, if you are romantically involved with one another" Whoa! Now we have a problem. When members of a congregation become romantically involved with each other's spouses, God will not be pleased.

"But I tell you, be romantically involved with your enemies." Naw, this isn't going to happen.

Romance is real. From culture to culture it varies in definition, but it is real. However, romance is not the love of God.

Preference as love

This will be a short one.

Do you love basketball, or do you love football more? Do you love pizza? Do you love New York? Do you love the smell in the air that follows after a rain? Do you love walks on the beach?

All of these actually represent a preference.

If you will tune your ears to the phrase, you will see how widespread is this usage of *love*. It illustrates the problem for Christians. We use the word *love* to mean so much that it no longer really means anything. That is why the illustration of the multitudes in the vineyard is so important. Read again this sentence: "We use the word *love* to mean so much that it no longer really means anything." So the multitudes live their whole lives ignorant of what God says is most important. Scary.

While we all have our preferences, and while our preferences of themselves are real and not evil, our preferences are not the same as is the love of God.

"But I tell you, prefer your enemies . . ." No, no, no! This is not the will of God. This is not the love of God. This is not the Great Commandment nor the New Commandment.

Physical intimacy as love

Does your spouse think you are a great lover? Should young Christians be married before they make love? You understand exactly what I am saying, but what we really are talking about is physical intimacy.

Physical intimacy is real and enjoyable and powerful. Of itself it is not bad nor evil. However, Christians cannot allow this definition of *love* to confuse them as to what the will of God is.

Are we to be physically intimate with God with all of our hearts and all of our souls and all of our strength? How, exactly, will you manage that?

"By this will all men know we are His disciples, because we are physically intimate with one another"? Perhaps God wants us to be physically intimate with our enemies?

46

Clearly, physical intimacy is real, but this is not what God means when He speaks of love.

Friendship as love

You probably have many friends. Some of them are better friends than are others. Like most people, you probably have several "best" friends. Blessed is the marriage in which husband and wife are best friends. Friendship is real.

The biblical word for friendship is *phileo*. It not only is real, it is God-ordained. But it is not the word the Great Commandment nor the New Commandment uses. It is not the word used when the Bible commands us to love our enemies. The love of God is expressed by the biblical word *agape*. *Phileo* "friendship" is real, but it is inadequate regarding obeying the Great Commandment, the New Commandment, and loving our enemies. Friendship does not fulfill the law. Friends occasionally sin against one another.

Accepting this distinction is quite important. Eventually you will have the opportunity to encourage one who has been physically, sexually or emotionally abused by another. Certainly counseling one who has suffered that he or she be friends with the abuser would not be right. Do not counsel the victim of continuing abuse to develop a warm, emotional attachment to his or her abuser because you think "God commands it". The victim will conclude that you are insane. This type of counseling is not Christian.

In our versions of the Bible friendship is *love* because that is the way it currently is translated. Friendship is real and has a wonderful place in our lives. Yet friendship is not the love of God that is our great priority.

Our culture has many different uses for the word *love*. They are all real. But none of them means what God means when He speaks of His greatest priority. The American meanings of *love* never will enable one to be more than an annoying nobody who gains nothing. To the Creator the great American lover is unimpressive.

Here is how our culture teaches our children about love. Two people prefer each other and become infatuated with each other. They treat each other romantically. They become physically intimate. For a while they are best friends. The real, but polluted, love that they enjoy continues to build for a while. It is real! If they are not mature in Christ, it is the most powerful thing they have experienced! But without the blessing of God it will not remain fulfilling. The nature of sin within them will destroy the relationship. Such a sequence of "loves" is great stuff for movies and novels, but life does not fit a Hollywood author's ending. Without exceptions life fits the Divine Author's ending.

Our cultural "pollution" of love is not pollution from the unbeliever's point of view. American cultural love is all that this unbelieving person has. From the point of view of human experience it is the best of what he or she has. As American Christians we know how the concept of American love is used, so we will understand what other Americans are saying. We can communicate with unbelieving Americans so that they can understand the gospel. American love is "pollution" when we interpret God's Great Commandment and New Commandment as if He is talking about American love. To interpret God's Word as if American love is the issue is tragic. We end up as annoying nobodies who gain nothing.

All of these meanings of *love* will not go away. Christians will not be able to change the way our society uses the word *love*. Christians will have to prepare themselves to live in both worlds. Pastors and churches will have to make the difference clear to their congregations. While we want to understand unbelievers, we as believers want to please God. We want to do what God says is most important. In thinking and living this way we will be both salt and light.

Nothing is inherently evil about the "polluted love" that Americans believe. Infatuation, romance, preference, physical intimacy, and friendship all are real. They only are "pollution" if you willingly choose to believe that they are the same as the love of God. They only are "pollution" if you let yourself continue to think they represent the love God requires. However, if you choose to believe God's definition of *love* and you willingly and purposefully love Him and others as your first priority, then the love of God will make your infatuation and romance holy. Your preferences become holy. Your physical intimacy and friendships become holy. The fact that obeying God results in holiness is not surprising.

While we have a problem with cultural pollution, we also have a divine solution.

Chapter 4

We Have a Divine Solution

And this is my prayer: that your love may abound more and more in knowledge and depth of insight, so that you may be able to discern what is best and may be pure and blameless until the day of Christ, filled with the fruit of righteousness that comes through Jesus Christ—to the glory and praise of God (Phil. 1:9-11).

Here is a passage that begins by emphasizing the growth of our love. The phrase "abound more and more" talks about the love of God. This seems redundant. If my love abounds, then it is plentiful. Love that abounds is everywhere and affects everything all the time.

Elsewhere we are told that God is holy. In a literal sense once is enough to convince us that God is holy. But when we are told, "Holy, holy, holy is the Lord God Almighty", we realize that God emphasizes His holiness to a magnificent degree.

So when the Apostle Paul prays that the love of Christians would abound more and more, he emphasizes to a magnificent degree the growth of love. Look at it as a promise. Your love can abound. Your love can abound more. Your love can abound more and more. If you believe it, you can choose it. If you choose it, you can achieve it, because God is highly motivated to grant increasing love to His children. God's love is God's great motivation. This always is the will of God for you. It is how we know who His disciples are. As our Father, He wants to impress on us His love.

This prayer for increasing love is not directed at increasing your emotional response. Notice that He wants our love to abound more and more in knowledge and depth of insight. Knowledge and depth of insight relate to thinking, not feeling. He wants your knowledge of love and your depth of insight about love to increase more and more. He wants you to think more and more.

Again look at this as a promise. Abounding love is yours when you decide you want it. The love of God·is a choice, not a feeling. You can learn it and practice it. You can become skillful at it. This is what cooperation with God is all about. The love of God is for active Christians who, on purpose, will love God and others. If I passively wait for God to make me feel love, I may wait a very long time. I may have to wait until I get to heaven. From an earthly perspective that is a wasted life.

Next the apostle shows us why he wants our love to abound more and more in knowledge and depth of insight. He wants us to discern what is best. Many moral values exist in the sight of God. Everything that He says is right, is righteous. Everything that He says is sin, is sinful. But some righteous things are more important than are other righteous things. We have a Great Commandment and we have a New Commandment. They are more important than is anything else. Love fulfills the Law.

If our love is abounding more and more in knowledge and depth of insight, then we can discern what is best. If our love is not abounding more and more in knowledge and depth of insight, then we cannot discern what is best. If my love is not growing in knowledge and depth of insight, then I am not growing. If I am not cooperating with the will of God, then I am rebelling against the will of God.

Remember the accurate synopsis of 1 Corinthians 13:1-3?

Without love I am an annoying nobody who gains nothing.

That sounds a lot like someone who does not discern what is best.

As the years and decades roll by, God's will is that you love Him and your neighbor with all your heart, all your soul, and all your mind. So use your mind. Think about what love is. Interpret the gospels by the theme that Jesus lived a life of love toward God, His neighbor, and even His enemies. Certainly He was sent to earth to seek and to save those who are lost. Love is how and why He did it. Certainly He was sent to redeem us by His sacrifice on the cross, but from the time He was born to the time He died, He, on purpose, loved the people of the world.

Jesus did more than die on the cross. He set the example of how to live after we have acknowledged Him as Lord and Savior.

Since *love* is the action word of the Great Commandment and the New Commandment, and since it is the first priority of God that fulfills all the Law and the Prophets, spend time praying that God will give you knowledge of the love of God and insight in how to apply the love of God.

After our knowledge and depth of insight into the love of God abounds, we can discern what is best. Then, knowing what to do and say in every situation, we can remain pure and blameless. Further, our love will enable those around us to remain more pure and more blameless, because our love will cover over a multitude of sins.

Abounding love works like this. Your patience is the needed solution when people are angry. Your unselfishness is the needed solution when people are selfish. Your kind and humble rejoicing in the truth is the solution when people are delighting in evil. Your protection and perseverance are the solution when people are biting and devouring one another.

> *. . . rather, serve one another in love. The entire law is summed up is a single command: "Love your neighbor as yourself." If you keep on biting and devouring each other, watch out or you will be destroyed by each other* (Gal. 5:13b-15).

Discerning what is best is done by thinking. God-inspired creativity and inspiration still emerge through your mind. As you live the life of love, you become more knowledgeable. Your experience combines with your knowledge to increase your depth of insight so that you can be pure and blameless. Over time the more you try, the more God teaches you. The more you succeed, the more opportunity He gives you. As you in your own life prove that "love never fails", the more influence you have over others. The more you influence others to obey the Great Commandment and the New Commandment, the more God is glorified through Jesus Christ. This is a win-win situation that continues until the day of Christ. After that, we are told that sin will not be a problem. After the day of Christ, we all, on purpose, will love. God is love; the love of God is an eternal absolute.

Remember that "God is love". If we intend to show the world the love of God, then we have a purposeful way to do it.

If we are "filled with the fruit of righteousness that comes through Jesus Christ", then we are "filled to the measure of all the fullness of God". While saying this is easier than doing it, it can be done. In fact, everyone who is a Christian can succeed at it—if you want it. And surprise, surprise! Being filled to the measure of all the fullness of God is a result of being rooted and established in the love of God.

And I pray that you, being rooted and established in love, may have power, together with all the saints, to grasp how wide and long and high and deep is the love of Christ, and to know this love, that surpasses knowledge—that you may be filled to the measure of all the fullness of God (Eph. 3:17b-19)

To be rooted in something requires considerable passage of time. To be established in something requires considerable passage of time. However, once we are rooted and established in love, we receive power to grasp the scope of the love of God. The more you have, the more you get. The more you give, the more you get. I am amazed that God sets no limits on how much of His love we can receive. He sets no limits on how much of His love we can give. I'm appalled that we don't seem to care. Perhaps this happens because we do not see the love of God as a practical solution to problems. Perhaps we prefer to think of love as "infatuation/romance/preference/physical intimacy/friendship". Perhaps we do not see the love of God as a component of all success. Perhaps we are so worldly that we would not recognize the love of God even if He became flesh and lived among us as an example. Say, now! That would be a problem!

Yet He says that being rooted and established in love will give us power to grasp the scope of the love of God. Certainly this includes understanding how much God loves us. We find great comfort and encouragement in the fact that God loves us. His love for you is on a scale so great that the dimensions of love (width, length, height, and depth) surpass knowledge. Since God is infinite and God is love; the love of God is infinite.

Probably someone somewhere will attempt to use this passage as an excuse to refuse to actively and thoughtfully, on purpose, love God. "Since the love of God surpasses knowledge, it cannot be known." But since God is infinite and we want to know Him, we, on purpose, continue to try to get to know Him. On purpose we talk to Him. He calls that *prayer*. On purpose we listen to Him; that is called *meditation*, a form of prayer. To get to know Him better we read His Word. The fact that God is infinite does not discourage us from trying to know Him. Rather it encourages us, because we have a precious relationship with a God who never will bore us nor stop amazing us.

The same thing is true with the love of God. Our knowledge and depth of insight into the love of God forever will remain a source of awe and gratitude. It never will bore us nor cease to amaze us. It always will be with us and always will inspire us. The love that surpasses knowledge is infinite, not unknowable. It is an awe-inspiring resource that never can be exhausted. It is, in fact, your limitless inheritance. Don't be too lazy to care.

So being rooted and established in love is a good thing. We receive power to grasp the scope of God's love. To "grasp" the love of God also means we can "get a handle" on the love of God. You can choose to use it. The love of God is a choice; it is a skill. On purpose you do it.

Once we grasp the scope of the love of God, because we are rooted and established in the love of God, we are filled to the measure of all the fullness of Christ.

God is the One Who sets the boundaries. God is the One Who commends and condemns. God is the One Who is wholly righteous. When He says you are doing well, you are doing well. When He says you can do something, then you better believe you can do it. And you can be filled to the measure of the fullness of Christ. You can be a pleasant somebody who gains something holy.

God is love. Whoever lives in love lives in God, and
God in him. Love is made complete among us so that
we will have confidence on the day of judgment,
because in this world we are like him (1 John 4:16-17).

Wow! We can have confidence on the day of judgment!

Wow! In this world we are like Him!

We are like Him because His love is made complete in us.
We are like Him because we are filled to the measure of all the
fullness of Christ. To be filled to the measure of all the fullness of Christ is another way of saying you will be like Him.
Jesus is the light of the world. Then He sends us out and calls
us the light of the world. God is love. He loves the world to
the point of sending Jesus to rescue us from sin. On His way
to the cross, Jesus lived a life of love. Then He tells us to love
our neighbors and even our enemies. We can be like Him. In
this world you can be like Him. If you can believe His words
instead of believing your culture, you can be like Him. If you
choose His plan for your future over your habitual traditions,
you can be like Him.

The love of God is a choice. On purpose you choose to
love. The love of God is not an emotional response. If I insist
on believing that the love of God is a feeling, then I passively
wait until God makes me "feel" like being Christlike. In the
meantime I will remain an annoying nobody who gains nothing.

By the love of God we know we are like Him. By the love
of God we know who His disciples are. God is love; He is not
an emotion. He is not a passion nor a sensation. God is not
infatuation. He is not romance. He is not preference nor physical intimacy. God is not friendship. God is love, but He

defines love His way. If you want to know God, you want to know what He says love is. If you want to know God, think, on purpose, about who He is.

> *Everyone who loves has been born of God and knows God. Whoever does not love does not know God, because God is love* (1 John 4:7b-8).

Consider John's words this way: "Everyone who, on purpose, chooses to love (God's way) has been born of God and knows God. Whoever does not, on purpose, choose to love (God's way) does not know God, because God is love (as He has defined *love*)". This is cause for serious contemplation.

Our Creator God became a human being—the Lord Jesus Christ. Since the Bible is a consistent whole, we can see that the love of God is the priority of the Messiah.

Chapter 5

The Love of God as the Son of God

Philip said, "Lord, show us the Father and that will be enough for us."

Jesus answered: "Don't you know me Philip, even after I have been among you such a long time? Anyone who has seen me has seen the Father. How can you say, 'Show us the Father'? Don't you believe that I am in the Father, and that the Father is in me? The words I say to you are not just my own. Rather, it is the Father, living in me, who is doing his work. Believe me when I say that I am in the Father and the Father is in me; or at least believe on the evidence of the miracles themselves" (John 14:8-11).

The Lord Jesus Christ is the Creator God who also became a human being. This is the conclusion the Spirit of God leads us to make. Many passages of Scripture point to the divinity of Jesus Christ. The above passage from the gospel of John records Jesus' appeal to the apostles to believe that He and the Father are one. He says, "At least believe on the evidence of the miracles themselves."

The miracles of Jesus Christ affected nature in such a dramatic and powerful way that He would have to be infinite God to accomplish them.

Jesus turned 120 gallons of water into wine. How did He do that? Certainly not by magic! To convert water into wine He rearranged the atoms and molecules untold trillions of times.

From the lunch of one person Jesus fed the multitudes. How did He do that? He had to create matter from nothing. Again, this requires the creation of billions of trillions of atoms arranged into molecules and then arranged into biological sequences that we call bread and fish. On purpose all of this had to be done, not by time and chance. Of course, that is no big deal for the One who created the heavens and the earth from nothing. He is the infinite God, not a Hollywood caricature.

Jesus calmed the stormy Sea of Galilee. How did He do that? He had to change the momentum of every molecule near the surface of the sea. He had to contact and change the momentum of every molecule in the winds and disburse the barometric pressure over the entire Middle East.

Jesus brought Lazarus back from the dead. How did He do that? He had to mend the cellular structure of virtually every cell in Lazarus' body, complete with genetic codes, and seat Lazarus' spirit back in a body that for four days had been dead. Our best surgeons can't even find the spirit.

Yes, believe in the evidence of the miracles themselves! The miracles required that the miracle worker be the infinite Creator God. Jesus performed the miracles to prove that He was the infinite Creator God.

Yet Jesus did more than miracles. He worked miracles lovingly. He demonstrated how to live a loving life. He was not sent to abolish the Law but to fulfill it. Loving God and our neighbors as ourselves fulfills the Law. On purpose Jesus fulfilled the Law. We also, on purpose, love God and our neighbor.

Now, note the verse that appears after John 14:8-11.

"I tell you the truth, anyone who has faith in me will do what I have been doing. He will do even greater things

than these because I am going to the Father. And I will do whatever you ask in my name, so that the Son may bring glory to the Father. You may ask me for anything in my name, and I will do it" (John 14:12-14).

He says, *"Anyone who has faith in me will do what I have been doing."* My experience with American Christianity leads me to conclude that a lot of sincere charlatans are working pitiful miracles, but virtually no one is working miracles on a par with those of Jesus Christ. If working miracles is a necessary companion to having faith in Christ, then at least we know that some of the apostles had faith in Christ, for they worked real miracles. We truly wonder about the rest of us!

Jesus said, "He will do even greater things than these . . .." The pitiful miracles that reportedly abound in American churches do not measure up. They are not even in the same league with the miracles of Jesus, let alone greater than what He was doing. What is going on? Don't we have faith in Him? Can outstanding miracles like those of Jesus go unrecognized?

If the context of Jesus' statement is left at John 14:11, then we all are in a world of hurt, with another world of hurt awaiting our arrival after we die.

However, if we go back to John 13:34-35 to establish the context of Jesus' words, then John 14:11 can be understood in light of the priorities of God.

"A new command I give you: Love one another. As I have loved you, so you must love one another. By this will all men know that you are my disciples, if you love one another" (John 13:34-35).

The doctrinal context of at least the next two chapters begins here. He directly stresses the New Commandment. As

He nears His sacrificial death, He stresses what is most important. Because He loves the apostles, He is telling them to love one another. He is giving them what they desperately need. He is stressing what fulfills the Law. He is treating the Great Commandment and the New Commandment as if they truly are God's priority. The same Holy Spirit who spoke through John in this passage also spoke through Paul in 1 Corinthians, chapters 12 and 13. Chapter 12 concludes with reference to apostles, prophets, miracles, healings, etcetera, and then refers to "the most excellent way". Chapter 13 defines this "most excellent way" as the love of God. The love of God is better than miracles are. Loving others with the love of God is better than is working miracles for them.

God so loved the world that He sent his Son. He commended His love toward us in that, while we were yet sinners, Christ died for us. Jesus Christ loved us as the Father loved us. Jesus loved us in word and deed exactly as the Father desired, because God is love. To see Jesus was to see the Father. To see Jesus was to see the love of God in human form—to see the example of a holy and righteous God who loved even His enemies.

If A=B, and B=C, then A=C. Remember? This is such an obvious fact. If God is love, and Jesus is God, then Jesus is love.

Jesus was righteous because He began as and remained a lover of God and others. He fulfilled the Law. To prove that He was God, He worked outstanding miracles. He said everything the Father told Him to say and did everything the Father told Him to do. And He did it all the way the Father told Him to do it. He loved God with all His heart, all His soul, all His strength, and all His mind. Either we believe this, or we believe that He gave us a command to do what He Himself would not do.

Let's again look at John 14:11.

"Believe me when I say that I am in the Father and the Father is in me; or at least believe on the evidence of the miracles themselves" (John 14:11).

To demonstrate that He is God, Jesus worked miracles. In the working of miracles He always was loving people, or He would have sinned by being "an annoying nobody who gains nothing".

Jesus worked miracles to demonstrate that He is divine. Perhaps we need to pretend to work miracles to demonstrate that we are divine. We don't know what love is, we certainly are not "rooted and established in love", but do we do miracles? This is worth pondering, because denominations do matter.

Jesus set the example of the greatest moral priorities. He actually fulfilled the Law. He lived a life of love. A miracle a day kept obscurity away, but every word and deed was a perfect example of loving God and His enemies. He drew crowds with His miracles; then He blessed them with the Word of God, lovingly delivered. Many individually sought Him for a miracle; He loved each person individually. Those who received a supernatural miracle that solved their problems with health, wealth, comfort, and convenience received only a temporary blessing. All soon were challenged with another trial concerning their health, wealth, comfort, and convenience. Most of them missed the eternal and precious blessing of seeing the love of God fulfilling the Law. Love could be theirs without limit, but they were satisfied with only animal comforts. A wicked and adulterous generation always seeks after signs and wonders.

The miracles Jesus worked took only moments to perform, but His hours were spent loving God and people. All the miracles Jesus worked in Israel could have been performed within 24 hours, but his 30-plus years all were spent loving people. To ask what Jesus had been doing on any given day most accurately could have been answered by the conclusion: He was loving people.

I tell you the truth, anyone who has faith in me will do what I have been doing. He will do even greater things than these, because I am going to the Father. And I will do whatever you ask in my name, so that the Son may bring glory to the Father. You may ask me for anything in my name, and I will do it (John 14:12-14).

The doctrinal context is the New Commandment. Everything God considers to be important hangs on the Commandment to love God and our neighbor. This is what Jesus lived. This is what He was doing. This is what He wanted to pass on. While the apostles and others truly worked outstanding miracles, they also spent only moments doing so. They spent much more time lovingly preaching and teaching the Word of God. They spent the vast majority of their time, in word and deed, loving God and others.

Jesus promised us that we would do the things that He was doing. He promised us that we would do even greater things than He had done. If this refers to His miracles, then we have little hope. If this refers to the New Commandment, then we have hope and ample confirmation.

But if anyone obeys his word, God's love is truly made complete in him. This is how we know we are in him: Whoever claims to live in him must walk as Jesus did (1 John 2:5-6).

*We know that we have passed from death to life,
because we love our brothers. Anyone who does not
love remains in death* (1 John 3:14).

*And so we know and rely on the love God has for us.
God is love. Whoever lives in love lives in God, and
God in him. In this way love is made complete among
us so that we will have confidence on the day of
judgment, because in this world we are like him*
(1 John 4:16-17).

"The things that I have been doing . . ." and *" . . . in this
world we are like him"*. What if the Great Commandment is to
love as Jesus loved instead of seeking after miracles? What if
we know who the true disciples of Jesus Christ are by their
love and not by a wicked and adulterous attempt to seek after
signs and wonders?

Miracles are available by the sovereign will of God.
Anything He has done, He can do again. Yet the priority of
God remains the love of God. We can dare to say it this way:

He told us the truth, anyone who has faith in Him will
love others as He has been loving others. He will love
more people for a longer time through His Spirit in us,
because He went to the Father. And He is enabling us
to do whatever loving work we do in His name, so that
He brings glory to the Father. We can ask Him to let
our love abound more and more in knowledge and
depth of insight so that we can discern what is best,
and He will do it.

We can ask Him for anything in His name, and He will do
it.

We know that what we ask of Him must be in accordance with His will. He is not the infinite genie who grants unlimited wishes but the Creator who began a good work in us and will bring it to completion.

The good work He begins in us is a loving work. As we humble ourselves before Him, He will lift us up in due time. As we become rooted and established in love, we can get a handle on how wide and long and high and deep is the love of God, that we may be filled to the measure of all the fullness of God.

If you believe it, you can choose it. If you choose it, you can achieve it. This is not true of everything, but it always is true of the will of God. Christians are destined to a loving hereafter. From the perspective of eternity the proverb would read, "When you believed it, you began to achieve it." So why wait?

We can ask Him for anything in His name, and He will do it. He is not more zealous to grant anything to us than He is that we obey the Great Commandment and the New Commandment. Is this true of your life? Is this true for your family? Do you have a long list of things God has done for you and through you during this past week? Do you want one?

Chapter 6

The Love of God
as the Blessing of God

"Do not be afraid, Abram. I am your shield, your very great reward" (Gen. 15:1b).

If you belong to Christ, then you are Abraham's seed, and heirs according to the promise (Gal. 3:29).

God is love (1 John 4:8b).

God is love. If you belong to Christ, then the love of God to you and through you is your very great reward. This is more practical and provable than is anything else in Scripture. When you have the eyes to see it and the ears to hear it, then it becomes apparent everywhere. Our previous blindness and deafness is revealed. A new depth of wisdom is discovered. Clear direction literally is unmistakable.

The theme of this chapter is quite simple. The love of God is the blessing of God. The mind boggles at the multitude of ways this can be seen. Meditating on all the ways that the love of God blesses you and those around you becomes a worshipful experience.

You can have all the love of God that you want. You can give it away to whoever you want. Then get more. Your supply is inexhaustible. God will see to this. God is zealous to motivate you and empower you to love Him and others.

Unfortunately prayer for blessing can be sincere yet shallow. Both Christianity and other religions have this one thing in common: They pray for health, wealth, comfort, and convenience. They pray for it more than they receive it.

Health, wealth, comfort, and convenience are fine things for which to pray. We all want them. In the American Christian context we explain it this way. Ask for health, wealth, comfort, and convenience in accordance with God's will. He will answer you in one of the following ways. His answer will be "yes", "no", or "not yet". This is all true and fine as far as it goes.

The vast majority of the time the answer is "no", but we pretend the answer is "not yet" and continue to pray away. We stick with it, because that is "faithfulness". After all:

You do not have, because you do not ask (James 4:2b).

So we ask and we seek and we knock and we persevere. For all the answers we receive, we sometimes feel as though we might as well be banging our heads into a block of wood. And if we are asking for the wrong thing, we might as well cover the block of wood with gold and recognize that the god we are serving is some idol, not the real God.

James continues:

 When you ask, you do not receive, because you ask with wrong motives, that you may spend what you get on your pleasures (Jas. 4:3).

The theme of the chapter is that the blessing of God is the love of God. Grasping this is important for Christians in America. Without choosing to discipline ourselves to a life that obeys the Great Commandment and the New Commandment, we are annoying nobodies who gain nothing. The love of God is a priority that can be lived. It is the Great Commandment. The on-purpose loving of God and your neighbor is not legalism, because it can and must be achieved. The Great Commandment and the New Commandment are not legalism; they are grace!

We know that the Law is good if we use it properly. It is intended to convict us of sin. And God empowers the law to convict us of sin. It works every time! The Law is not intended to impart righteousness. Through our faith in the blood of our Savior Jesus Christ and His resurrection as Lord, we receive righteousness. The Great Commandment and the New Commandment are not designed to convict us of sin. They are designed to be obeyed. God wants you to cooperate. Loving God and others is the most excellent way.

Begin asking God to bless you with the ability to love Him and others. Do this in the conscious awareness that God has defined what He means by love. The American version of love will not work. God wants something specific; you will not please Him by choosing to embrace the polluted definitions of love used in America. To direct all your heart, all your soul, all your strength, and all your mind toward infatuation, romance, preference, physical intimacy, and friendship is not the Great Commandment. It is a huge mistake. Take God seriously.

Love is patient, love is kind. It does not envy, it does not boast, it is not proud. It is not rude, it is not self-seeking, it is not easily angered, it keeps no record of wrongs. Love does not delight in evil but rejoices with the truth. It always protects, always trusts, always hopes, always perseveres. Love never fails (1 Cor. 13:4-8a).

Pray for the love of God. Pray for the wisdom to see God's love for you. Pray for the virtue of being loving toward God. Pray that your desires and your mind will cooperate with each other so you will be loving to your spouse and family.

Pray directly for the "components" of love. Ask for patience. Seek kindness. Since God decided this is important enough to define His love in these terms, it is important enough for you to ask for love in these terms.

As you experience the love of God toward you, thank Him for it. Praise Him for the love you receive from Him and others. Such love is not coincidence. He is at work. This is what He does in the life of a Christian. This is what Christianity is all about. These columns are based on God's definition of *love*.

Love is:	Love is not:
Patient	Easily annoyed
Kind	Mean
Content	Envious
Modest	Boastful
Humble	Proud
Polite	Rude
Unselfish	Self-seeking
Self-controlled	Easily angered
Forgiving	Revengeful
Rejoices with the truth	Delights in evil
Always protects	Causes harm
Always trusts	Cynical
Always hopes	Despairing
Always perseveres	Procrastinating
Succeeds	Fails

All the spiritual jewels in the left column are yours. Take all you want. This always is God's will for you. These spiritual qualities are yours in abundance. All you have to do is believe it, begin asking, and begin trying. The blessings will follow.

As you become rooted in love, God establishes love in your character in this way:

You become patient, kind, content, modest, humble, polite, unselfish, self-controlled, forgiving, joyful in the truth, protecting, able to build trust, hopeful, persevering, and successful.

Money cannot buy this. God will give this freely, continually, and increasingly. Your cup will run over. This is the spiritual treasure that God offers without limit in this world. How can you not value such an offer? Do you treasure something else in this world? Where your treasure is, there your heart will be also.

The fact that mature, skilled, loving people will get jobs and then promotions is self-evident. Such people will be given opportunity and then more opportunities. Your righteousness will rise like the dawn. The cause for which you stand will be bright as the noonday sun. You become a pleasant somebody who accomplishes much.

No matter how sincere we are, in comparison American love is rubbish. Without the love of God, sin will ruin infatuation, romance, preference, physical intimacy, and friendship. Eventually, no matter how much you "feel love", the sinful nature will produce sin in our lives. One or more of the following characteristics will be expressed:

You become easily annoyed, mean, envious, boastful, proud, rude, selfish, angry, revengeful, evil, harmful, cynical, full of despair, you give up, and/or you fail.

Any one of these traits can ruin your relationships. While, with the love of God, you always can make things better, without the love of God you always will make things worse. Any one of these components can keep you from getting hired. Even a brief occurrence can keep you from getting promoted.

Sin can get you fired and reduce or eliminate your opportunities. Admittedly the expression of these sins can feel good sometimes. Of course, you still are destroying relationships and opportunities, but you do feel good about it. You have received your reward.

So Christians have two alternatives. Choose the right one, or receive the wrong one by default. Know also that whichever you choose will become habitual and grow stronger. So choose the abundant life; virtue is in your future.

Do you want your love to abound more and more in knowledge and depth of insight so that you can discern what is best and be pure and blameless until the day of Christ? Ask for it. The answer always is "yes". You never will get a "no" or a "not yet". The answer always is "yes, as much as you want, right now, this very second." You even will be offered more than that for which you ask. Give love all the time.

> "Give, and it will be given to you. A good measure,
> pressed down, shaken together and running over, will
> be poured into your lap. For with the measure you use,
> it will be measured to you" (Luke 6:38).

If God is your very great reward, and God is love, then apply this verse and be rewarded. Apply this verse and be the reward of God to others. The love of God is the blessing of God. If you do not agree, then keep applying this passage to health, wealth, comfort, and convenience. See what it gets you.

At the same time, God insists that you take all the treasure, not just selected parts. Demanding a glutton's feast on the truth of the Word of God while you neglect patience and unselfishness is sin. He will not allow it. God declares that it is all part of the Great Commandment, so ask for it all. God says that He is love. You wouldn't dream of asking for just part of God, would you? Ask for it all. If you ask for it all, it is not greed, because God will see to it that you get the unselfishness that you need so that you are not greedy. Trust Him, because He has been building Christlike people for a long time.

Consider these passages as if the love of God is what is being asked for:

> *"And I will do whatever you ask in my name, so that*
> *the Son may bring glory to the Father. You may ask me*
> *for anything in my name, and I will do it"*
> (John 14:13-14).

Since God is love and you are loving, you reveal the glory of God.

> *"So do not worry, saying, 'What shall we eat?' or*
> *'What shall we wear?' For the pagans run after all*
> *these things, and your heavenly Father knows that you*
> *need them. But seek first his kingdom and his*
> *righteousness, and all these things will be given to you*
> *as well"* (Matt. 6:31-33).

Since God is love, is not the kingdom of God the kingdom of love? Seek the kingdom; everything else will be given you..

> *"Ask and it will be given to you; seek and you will*
> *find; knock and the door will be opened to you. For*
> *everyone who asks receives; he who seeks finds; and to*
> *him who knocks, the door will be opened. Which of*
> *you, if his son asks for bread, will give him a stone? Or*
> *if he asks for a fish, will give him a snake? If you, then,*
> *though you are evil, know how to give good gifts to*
> *your children, how much more will your Father in*

heaven give good gifts to those who ask him! So in
everything, do to others what you would have them do
to you, for this sums up the Law and the Prophets"
(Matt. 7:7-12).

What sums up the Law and the Prophets? The love of God
on which all the Law and the Prophets hang.

"If you remain in me, and my words remain in you, ask
whatever you wish, and it will be given you"
(John 15:7).

If your desire and choices remain in Him who is love, and
you remember and cooperate with all He has said, then ask for
whatever you wish. You will receive it.

This is the confidence we have in approaching God;
that if we ask anything according to his will, he hears
us. And if we know that he hears us—whatever we
ask—we know that we have what we asked of him
(1 John 5:14-15).

What possibly could be more in accordance with His will
than are the Great Commandment and the New Commandment? When you love the way God wants, and your eyes and
ears see Him at work in you and all around you, your confidence will be unshakable.

The love of God is the blessing of God. In comparison all
other blessings are minor. The Creator still can work any
supernatural miracle that He desires. He has not grown weak.
Because He has not grown weak, He also can transform you
into a lover of God and people. He will immerse you in the
love of the Father and the Son and the Holy Spirit.

Chapter 7

The Love of God
and the Filling of the Holy Spirit

*Jesus replied, "If anyone loves me, he will obey my
teaching. My Father will love him, and we will come to him
and make our home with him . . .. These words you hear are
not my own; they belong to the Father who sent me.*

*"All this I have spoken while still with you. But the
Counselor, the Holy Spirit, whom the Father will send in my
name, will teach you all things and will remind you of
everything I have said to you"* (John 14:23, 24b-26).

Love is the first priority of God and fulfills the Law.
Loving God is obeying Him. Loving God with all your heart
and all your soul and all your mind is obeying God with all
your heart, all your soul, and all your mind. When we are
ready to begin, the Father and the Son make their home with
us. Since the Father and the Son and the Holy Spirit are one,
the Father and the Son make their home with us in the person
of the Holy Spirit. He lives in us.

The Holy Spirit is called the Counselor; He teaches us.
Elsewhere He is called the Guide. How does He counsel us,
teach us, and guide us? The influence of the Holy Spirit
always is a loving influence. This is a good way to discern
whether our intuition is the voice of the Spirit or something
else.

How do you talk to yourself inside? Are you rude? Do you
listen to internal guilt, anger, and hopelessness? That is not the

Holy Spirit. The Holy Spirit loves you as the Father and the Son love you. He may cause you to think about guilt and anger, but He will do so kindly, patiently, unselfishly, and politely. Otherwise, He would not be cooperating with God's Great Commandment. The Holy Spirit is not an annoying nobody who gains nothing. He is a pleasant somebody who gains much.

The Holy Spirit will guide us, teach us, and counsel us to be loving the way God says we should be loving. Since that is the Father's first priority and the Son's first priority, it must be the Spirit's first priority. They are one.

> *"But when he, the Spirit of truth comes, he will guide you into all truth. He will not speak on his own; he will speak only what he hears, and he will tell you what is yet to come. He will bring glory to me by taking from what is mine and making it known to you"*
> (John 16:13-14).

The Father, the Son, and the Holy Spirit are one. The Spirit of truth tells us what the Father wants. He follows the Father's lead. The Father's priorities are the Spirit's priorities. Our experience of living with the Holy Spirit—being indwelt by the Father and the Son who have made their home with us— will be loving God and others with all our hearts, all our souls, and all our minds. Thinking that the Holy Spirit does not place a Holy priority on the Great Commandment and the New Commandment is absurd. The Father, the Son, and the Holy Spirit are one.

The Holy Spirit, also called the Spirit of truth, reminds us of everything Jesus has said to us. Not only does the Spirit remind us of what is true, He reminds us of what is most important. The Spirit who guides us does not want us to be annoying nobodies who gain nothing. He counsels us to be pleasant somebodies who gain everything. What a Comforter! As we fulfill the Law by living the love of God, we are bringing glory to our Lord Jesus Christ. This is one way the Holy Spirit brings glory to the name of Jesus. As we are like Jesus in this world, people can see that He is in us.

Dear friends, do not believe every spirit, but test the spirits to see whether they are from God (1 John 4:1a).

A lot of opinions exist in America about what the filling of the Spirit looks like. What is this experience? How does it feel? How do I test the spirits? Is this verse referring to the Holy Spirit or demon spirits or to the human spirit? The answer is "Yes". It refers to all spirits. While the Holy Spirit always will be loving, all other spirits sin by being unloving on occasion. The more unloving the spirit, the more evil it is. This is true of both demon spirits and human spirits.

In the same way that breaking one command of the Law breaks all the Law, violating even one component of God's love makes the word, thought, or deed unloving. Holiness is a perfect standard without any impurities. Those who do not belong to Christ on occasion can love others with what appears to be the love of God. Even though humanity is now sinful, we were designed as the image of God.

"If you love those who love you, what reward will you get? Are not even the tax collectors doing that?" (Matt. 5:46).

A person can, on occasion, love others with the love of God even before he or she becomes a Christian. This especially is true of an unbeliever who returns the occasional love of another unbeliever. Being forgiving to those who forgive you or protecting those who protect you is possible.

The love of God, like the Law of Moses, is all or nothing. Accept love as God defines it, not as we prefer it.

For example the world exhibits some patience. Occasional kindness is seen. Many cultures truly are polite. But Jesus is the Way, the Truth, and the Life. Love rejoices in the truth. To appear patient, kind, and polite but to refuse Jesus as personal Lord and Savior is rejecting the truth and not rejoicing in the truth at all. Since love rejoices in the truth, those who do not rejoice in the truth are not obeying God. God says, "*Love rejoices in the truth.*" According to God's definition of *love*, such people are not loving. Human sincerity is not the issue. The love of God is the issue. God says that love rejoices in the truth.

We can note that rejoicing in the truth is the only component of love that is bound to an emotional reaction. We either rejoice in the truth, or we delight in evil. Those who rejoice in their opinion of why they can ignore the plain-sense meaning of Scripture are fooling themselves; they really are delighting in evil. Faithfulness is defined by what we believe of Scripture. Those who are noteworthy by what they disbelieve are not faithful. How some can become famous "Christians" by proclaiming what they don't believe is amazing.

In this way Satan can appear as an angel of light. His priorities are lying, accusing, and tempting people to doubt God's words, but through the appearance of love he will disguise his goals. Emotions can appear similar to the love of God. Sincere emotions can overwhelm those who have not chosen mind over emotional desires. Animals use their minds only to execute their emotional desires.

This also is the way of wolves in sheep's clothing. While they have a form of godliness, they deny its power. Sincerely believing they are right, they do not know or care about the Great Commandment and the New Commandment. They generally are more interested in power and fame.

Remember that most American Christians love indirectly, as a babe in Christ would. Just because they do not know directly what love is does not make them lost. It just means that they are a lot less mature (and effective) than they could be. They have no good excuse for denying the most direct way to obey God. We have no other Great Commandment.

Trying the spirits takes time. When a person rejoices in the truth of God's Word (*all* of God's Word), then Christian trust can be built with that person. When the person continues to return the love of God toward those who are unloving, then more trust is built. When a person continues to love others over an extended period of time, regardless of how he or she is treated, then trust continues to build. When the person becomes better and better at loving others, then growth is observed.

Eventually you can trust that the person is a true disciple of Jesus Christ because such an individual has love for others, regardless of how the person is being treated. This is how to discern whether or not a spirit is of God. This is the fulfillment of the New Commandment.

> "*A new command I give you: Love one another. As I have loved you, so you must love one another. By this will all men know that you are my disciples, if you love one another*" (John 13:34-35).

We can know who the disciples of Jesus Christ are, because they love each other. They love even their enemies.

So what is this experience of being filled with the Spirit? What does it look like? How does it feel?

When you are filled with the Spirit, you experience a spontaneous desire to love others. As time goes on, you, on purpose, learn to love God and others. We do not remain mindless infants. God is looking for active minds, not limp ones. Thinking is spiritual.

When a person is born again, the Holy Spirit takes up residence in him or her. The indwelling of the Spirit at the moment of salvation can be calm or emotional. How this occurs has a lot to do with the desperation of the life from which the new Christian has just been saved. Infatuation even affects us in our salvation. Remember that truth, not emotional infatuation, is the issue. Enjoy your emotional responses, but don't subject your sanity to them.

When one is filled with the Spirit, Jesus causes the person to love others. You see the person being patient, unselfish, humble, forgiving, and everything else that God says is love. You see the person behaving as if he or she has been forgiven by a Holy God—as if the individual no longer carries around a burden of guilt. You see the person with hope and faith in what God has said—*all* of what God has said.

How does the filling of the Spirit feel? People experience this in different ways. Those who are relieved of a huge burden of guilt or despair may cry. Those who sense that God is near and that they, after years of seeking Him, are close to meeting Him after years of seeking Him may be elated. People who tend to be emotional will be emotional. People who often are not emotional may not display emotion at all.

The number-one sign that a person is filled with the Holy Spirit is that the person is holy. A holy babe in Christ may know little and, on purpose, be slow to love mean people. Those who know little and who, on purpose, struggle to love God and others still are babes in Christ. When a babe in Christ, on purpose, is slow to love over the years, then the person is spending a lot of time quenching the Holy Spirit. Remember that the Holy Spirit, who is kind and patient (loving), lets us move at the pace we choose.

We feel sad when we realize that brothers or sisters in Christ are stunting their own growth and blessing. They sincerely may believe they are leaders in the church. However, without on-purpose loving, their real motivations will be power and fame. Without on-purpose loving, they actually will be annoying nobodies who gain nothing. Even deciding whether they are Christians or wolves in sheep's clothing may be difficult. Fortunately, God has given us direction on how to treat them.

We are to love people. Whether they love us back is not the issue. We love our enemies whether they treat us good or bad. We love Christians whether they treat us good or bad. We never have a time in which being unloving is justified. No matter how great the trial, the moment we sin against a person by being unloving, we have become part of the problem, not the solution. Love never fails. When you are loving, you are accomplishing all that God intends to be accomplished. You are a pleasant somebody who gains everything. The world already has enough annoying nobodies who gain nothing.

As the Holy Spirit fills us, He grants spiritual gifts through Christians. This also is a topic of much debate in America. Into this debate let's inject the Great Commandment and the New Commandment.

Now to each one the manifestation of the Spirit is given for the common good (1 Cor. 12:7).

Spiritual gifts are not magical powers that we receive to use as we wish. The gifts are the Holy Spirit Himself and serve those around us through our cooperation with Him. The gifts are for the common good. That is not surprising, since love is not self-seeking.

1 Corinthians 12 continues discussing the body of Christ and describing the spiritual gifts. The chapter concludes in this way:

And now I will show you the most excellent way (1 Cor. 12:31b).

Immediately the Spirit teaches us that no matter what we say, think, or do, if we do not express it in love, we are annoying nobodies who gain nothing. Then the Spirit goes on to define what *love* is. Love is the most excellent way. It is the Great Commandment and the New Commandment. It is more important than are any of the spiritual gifts. Love must occur first.

Perhaps the Spirit will not empower annoying nobodies to gain nothing. Supposing that the Spirit of God would enable supernatural influence to be directed by unloving people is absurd. Supposing that God wants spiritual babes to lead the church with supernatural power is absurd. What benefit happens in gifting an annoying person so that person can be supernaturally annoying?

Why does the American church constantly emphasize the spiritual gifts and neglect the true emphasis of the love of God? Seeking supernatural power without becoming rooted and established in the love of God is more like witchcraft than it is Christianity. Clearly and repetitively God's Word tells us that love is the first priority. Love is the most excellent way. How can we, as American Christians, ignore this?

"Why do you call me 'Lord, Lord,' and do not do what I say?" (Luke 6:46).

Why, indeed, do we call Him "Lord" and then ignore what He says is most important? Part of the reason is wickedness.

"Because of the increase in wickedness, the love of most will grow cold . . ." (Matt. 24:12).

Another reason is that the worries of this world and the deceitfulness of wealth choke the word and make it unfruitful (Matt. 13:22). The eternal treasure that God has made available to us is the love of God. Obviously that is not what we really want. We are in severe danger of judgment.

The Comforter—the Holy Spirit—teaches us and guides us according to the will of God. The Holy Spirit empowers us to love. Love is the most excellent way. Nothing Christian can be accomplished without it.

Seek as your treasure the love of God. Seek the love of God as you seek God Himself, for God is love. Dare to question mindless, selfish, and unthinking assertions of spiritual power. Don't let your thinking become clouded by assertions of emotional highs.

Therefore, do not be foolish, but understand what the Lord's will is. Do not get drunk on wine, which leads to debauchery. Instead, by filled with the Spirit (Eph. 5:17-18).

Perhaps you are ready for a change.

Chapter 8

The Love of God
and Repentance

From that time on Jesus began to preach, "Repent, for the kingdom of heaven is near" (Matthew 4:17).

Repentance is well-understood as a 180-degree change in our attitudes and behaviors. John the Baptist preached repentance, as did Peter, Paul, and Jesus. Noah was a preacher of righteousness and called on the people of his day to repent. Moses and the prophets called for repentance.

From the human perspective the Holy Spirit brings us to the point of repentance. At that time we humble ourselves and admit our sin. The infinite Creator God is adamant about this. He has thought everything through with infinite detail an infinite number of times. He is convinced that He absolutely is correct in His conclusions. Admitting our sin is non-negotiable. This will bring us to the realization that we deserve eternal punishment and that we can do nothing to redeem ourselves.

Provided we recognize that Jesus Christ is the infinite God who paid for our sins on the cross with His own blood, we dare to have hope. If we continue to humble ourselves and submit to Jesus as our Savior and Lord, He will cause us to be born again into His kingdom. Jesus Christ is risen from the dead, He is alive, and He is King. We may realize all of this so quickly and gently that we don't realize all that is going on. Nevertheless during this time we change our attitudes about

Jesus Christ; then, He changes us, so that with His help we can change our actions.

From God's point of view (which a saved person readily accepts), even our faith is a gift of God. Without His initiating a call to repent, we never could see past our spiritual blindness.

From the human point of view, if you are drawn to repent, then you are responsible for humbling yourself. Humbling ourselves requires being aware of the righteousness and infinite power of God and of His absolute right to do anything He wants to do with us. Such humility pleases God.

"This is the one I esteem: he who is humble and contrite in spirit, and trembles at my word" (Isa. 66:2b).

When we repent, our spirits are ready to begin doing what is right. Our spirits are ready to do what God says is most important. We do not continue to doubt and waver in our intention to please Him. The fear of God is the beginning of wisdom; we tremble at His words. This is normal for a Christian.

Christians recognize that the Bible is God's Word and that faith in God and faith in His word essentially are the same. While Jesus Christ is more than the Bible, He is not less than the Bible. Believing the Word of God is believing God. That is why our lives change.

And we also thank God continually because, when you received the word of God, which you heard from us, you accepted it not as the word of men, but as it actually is, the word of God, which is at work in you who believe (1 Thess. 2:13).

The Word of God is at work in those who believe. The Word of God is not at work, in a redemptive sense, in those who do not believe.

Repentance is well-understood as a 180-degree change in behavior. We turn from what God calls *sin* and intend to live a righteous life. From God's perspective He insists that we cooperate with Him. We are passive in the creative act of becoming born again. But repentance is not passive; it is active. Repentance purposely is done, or it is not done at all.

Often people are willing to repent from sin and willing to accept Jesus as Lord and Savior but are confused as to what repentance actually is. Having been convicted by the Law, we know "from" what to repent, but we are not clear "to" what we repent. The new believer stops sinning as fast as he or she can identify what the sins are. The new Christian is zealous not to sin and is active in sharing the gospel with whoever will listen. This truly is a born-again occurrence. But long term, it may not be a lasting repentance.

Sometimes a new Christian indirectly will learn what righteousness is. Sometimes the new believer will grow unstintingly. Yet sometimes the babe in Christ will not be encouraged and not be directed into a proven repentance.

" . . . *I preached that they should repent and turn to God and prove their repentance by their deeds*" (Acts 26:20).

If a new Christian is not guided into bringing forth deeds in keeping with repentance, then disaster can result. Pleasing God by trying not to sin is impossible. When the Law is the only proactive instruction available, it kills.

Since loving God and your neighbor fulfills the Law, and since doing so is the Great Commandment, this is the first thing to teach the new believer. Nothing does a new believer more good.

> " . . . *the only thing that counts is faith expressing itself through love*" (Gal. 5:6).

> *The entire law is summed up in a single command; "Love your neighbor as yourself"* (Gal. 5:14).

Christians who care about God's priority teach new Christians how to repent to the point of bringing forth fruit in keeping with repentance. Since the love of God fulfills the law and sin is breaking the law, then on-purpose loving always is the goal of repentance. On-purpose loving is the proof of our repentance. We repent from sin, through our Lord Jesus Christ, to active cooperation with the Father and the Son and the Spirit in loving God and people God's way. When the Great Commandment is the proactive instruction available, it gives life. This is the most excellent way; anything less is sinful.

If my repentance consists only of trying to avoid sin, then I have not moved 180 degrees; I only have moved 90 degrees. My failure in the future is assured. Since I am not loving in my words, thoughts, and deeds, I am an annoying nobody who will gain nothing. Sure, I am trying not to sin. All my efforts result in my being an annoying nobody who gains nothing. Since the on-purpose loving of people God's way is done *on purpose*, and I don't know what, *on purpose*, to do, I am severely handicapped. Unless I, *on purpose*, learn to love God and others, I will waste much of my time on this earth.

Not only is a new believer in danger from lack of direction, the new believer also is in danger from being directed poorly. If he or she is guided into participation in a church program where few or no Christians, on purpose, love, he or she soon will become offended. By example this person will learn to offend. In a short while this man or woman will realize that all the promises read from the pulpit don't quite pan out as they are explained. All disappointment springs from false expectations. When Christians are told of all the blessings of God and never are taught nor encouraged to take the Great Commandment literally and seriously, then disappointment is assured. I wonder how many people who visit a church only once think that said church is a bunch of annoying nobodies who gain nothing.

Why not teach new Christians the Great Commandment? Why not get them started on the most direct path to pleasing God? Why not assure them that they, on purpose, can try? Why not show them the most excellent way?

Attempting to obey the Law will kill. God says so. Are we so offended by trying to obey that we mindlessly default to thinking that the Great Commandment also kills? Are we so passive in our faith that we do not cooperate with our Creator and His priority? Have we forgotten that to obey is better than sacrifice?

Honest Christians seem to be reluctant to urge other Christians, on purpose, to try. This happens because most Christians, on purpose, have tried to achieve human program after human program. Unfortunately we confuse the blessing of God with the imagined results we can achieve through a logical plan. We imagine what we want and determine what we need to do to achieve it. This seems reasonable because it is reasonable. However God is serious about the Great Commandment. He is convinced that love is better than are our plans and programs. Since God is serious about the Great Commandment, the blessing He wants to send is not sent. The love of God is the primary blessing of God. We do not want it. We are the losers.

In the church, any plan to organize and achieve any worthy goal truly is better than having no plan at all. This is absolutely true. But unless the love of God is the great cooperative priority during the application of the plan, the results God promises will not be achieved. God is highly motivated to bless pleasant somebodies who can gain everything. God will not bless annoying nobodies who will gain nothing. Those who do not, on purpose, love do not succeed at loving very well, if at all. Not loving God and others is sin.

The plans and programs often, in themselves, are not sinful. They are sinful only when the love of God is not the priority of the people involved in the plan. The love of God, if given the highest priority, will make your plans and programs holy.

What can we do? Teach new Christians the Great Commandment and the New Commandment. Live it yourself. If you never have understood what love is and therefore never have tried, on purpose, to love God and others, then admit your failure as sin and repent. Your past repentance only attained 90 degrees. Even if you intended a 180-degree repentance, if you did not love God with all your heart, all of your soul, and all of your mind, then your "fruit in keeping with repentance" never matured. Call sin what it is. God is faithful and will purify you of all unrighteousness. Commit to memory 1 Corinthians 13:4-8. On purpose do it. Apply it to everything you do. Really love God with all your heart and all your soul and all your mind. Watch the difference that doing this makes. It is the difference between indirect, occasional, and incidental blessing, and in direct, constant, and purposeful blessing. You will see for yourself.

Use a program to serve the needs of your church. Cooperate lovingly in implementing the plan. Look for the difference between an implemented program without conscious love and an implemented program with conscious love. The difference will be obvious. The results will be obvious. Praise God every time you see someone, on purpose, love another person. What you observe literally is God at work. Follow the leadership of those who are most mature at loving others. Love those who have authority but do not love others; that is the best way to change them. Pray that God will give them the precious gift of repentance, for repentance is a gift. Humbly treasure the gift of repentance that you received. What would we do without it?

> *And the Lord's servant must not quarrel; instead, he must be kind to everyone, able to teach, not resentful. Those who oppose him he must gently instruct, in the hope that God will grant them repentance leading them to the knowledge of the truth . . . (2 Tim. 2:24-25).*

Pray for the precious gift of repentance. Apart from the active participation of Jesus Christ in our lives, we can do nothing. As you recognize the truth of God's Word, humble yourself and admit it is true. Get rid of the decay that accompanies an unrepentant life.

> *Therefore, get rid of all the moral filth and the evil that is so prevalent and humbly accept the word planted in you, which can save you (Jas. 1:21).*

James was writing to Christians. This promise is not talking about salvation from hell but salvation from a life that is self-deceived because the Word is known but ignored. The very next verse says:

> *Do not merely listen to the word and so deceive yourselves. Do what it says (Jas. 1:22).*

We have a Great Commandment and a New Commandment; give them proper cooperation. This is good news and not guilt. This is your birthright as a Christian and not another disappointing program. This is the blessing of God. This is the abundant life. This is the most excellent way.

God is serious about His priorities. He will bless or curse in direct proportion to our faithfulness to the Great Commandment. Diligent work and perseverance are not enough. Recognizing and refusing to cooperate with false doctrine is not enough. Enduring hardship and remaining zealous for His name is not enough. Hating arrogance is not enough. You have no substitute for loving God and your neighbor with all your heart, soul, strength, and mind. If a church refuses to cooperate with Him, God eventually will put an end to that church. Revelation 2:1-7 lists as achievements of the Ephesian church all the deeds this paragraph mentions. Yet Jesus said:

> *"Yet I hold this against you; You have forsaken your first love. Remember the height from which you have fallen! Repent and do the things you did at first. If you do not repent, I will come to you and remove your lampstand from its place"* (Rev. 2:4, 5).

The Ephesian church had forsaken its first love. Bible-believing Christians always choose the plain-sense meaning of Scripture unless they find biblical reasons not to do so.

The church forsook its first love. We have no good reason to believe its first love was evangelism or any other truth. The best interpretation is that it forsook the love of God. The Ephesians no longer, on purpose, obeyed the Great Commandment.

Jesus actually told the people that He held it against them! Read it again: He held it against them! Sin kills churches. God is patient, but He will not be mocked. He is serious about love. Love is even greater than faith.

> *And now these three remain: faith, hope and love. But the greatest of these is love* (1 Cor. 13:13).

Bible-believing American Christians: realize that a church cannot survive the presence of Jesus Christ if you forsake your faith in God. Faith in what God says is an eternal absolute. Love is an eternal absolute that is greater than faith (1 Cor. 13:13). Therefore realize that forsaking the love of God is worse even than is forsaking the plain-sense meaning of Scripture.

The loving God who calls us to His eternal glory provides a way of salvation for those who humbly accept the Word planted in them. That Word can save them. The threat to the Ephesian church was not exclusive to the Ephesians.

> *"He who has an ear, let him hear what the Spirit says to the churches. To him who overcomes, I will give the right to eat from the tree of life, which is in the paradise of God"* (Rev. 2:7).

No guarantee exists for the survival of an unloving church. The guarantee is provided to the individual who overcomes. We overcome by remembering the love from which we have fallen, by repenting, and by loving God and others. This happens to be the best thing you can do in an unloving church. It also is the best thing you can do in a loving church.

What can we conclude from the love of God and repentance?

With the Apostle Paul we can rejoice that Jesus is preached in our churches, whether from false motive or true (Jesus often is preached unlovingly). Piled heaps of harvested grapes are better than are fewer grapes.

We can be assured that God's Word accomplishes exactly that for which He sent it.

We can maintain our repentance from sin by making the on-purpose loving of God and others as our highest personal priority.

Living the Great Commandment and the New Commandment requires discipline. Fortunately Jesus Christ is looking for disciples; that is our Great Commission.

Chapter 9

The Love of God
and the Great Commission

Then Jesus came to them and said, "All authority in heaven and on earth has been given to me. Therefore, go and make disciples of all nations, baptizing them in the name of the Father and of the Son and of the Holy Spirit, and teaching them to obey everything I have commanded you. And surely I am with you always, to the very end of the age" (Matt. 28:18-20).

Make no mistake about it; I am a Great-Commission Christian! Nothing in this book is opposed to sharing the gospel with the lost. Nothing is this book is intended to reduce our efforts to share the gospel locally and around the world.

Plans and programs

To accomplish many tasks Christians organize themselves in many ways. We have denominations, boards, agencies, para-church groups, committees, and teams. The list is long and ever-changing. Many truly can do some things better than a few can. All of us together share some tasks. Tasks that involve cooperation require planning, whether the job is local or global. Telling the world about the Lord Jesus Christ is both local and global. This is a mission that our Creator and King has given to all of us; it is the Great Commission. The plans and programs of all the various groups are myriad. All of the plans and programs have both strengths and weaknesses. Is one plan superior to all the others? No, I don't think so. However, does a most excellent way exist? God says, "Yes".

The love of God is the most excellent way. If your plan to lead the lost to salvation through Christ is a one-on-one plan, then doing so lovingly assures God's empowerment of your efforts. If your small group wants to invite visitors so that you can lead them to Christ through friendship evangelism, then a loving small group assures God's cooperation. If you prefer churchwide efforts such as revivals or block parties, then a loving congregation magnifies the gospel. The fact that an annoying nobody who gains nothing will not have the blessing of the omnipresent God likely will be self-evident. On the contrary, since "love is not proud", and "God opposes the proud", He has made rather obvious how He will respond. However, if our love abounds more and more in knowledge and depth of insight, then we can discern what is best and be pure and blameless until the day of Christ. We can be filled with the fruit of righteousness that we have through Jesus Christ (Phil. 1:9-11). Certainly being filled with the fruit of righteousness that we have through Jesus Christ is a manifestation of the Holy Spirit's power for us to be witnesses (Acts 1:8)!

Two variables determine the extent of our harvest as we share the gospel and seek to make disciples of the nations. The first is the sovereign will of God that can be viewed from the perspective of grace. Regardless of motive, the message of the gospel can be effective.

It is true that some preach Christ out of envy and rivalry, but others do so out of goodwill. The latter do so in love, knowing that I am put here for the defense of the gospel. The former preach Christ out of selfish

ambition, not sincerely, supposing that they can stir up
trouble for me while I am in chains. But what does it
matter? The important thing is that in every way,
whether from false motives or true, Christ is preached.
And because of this I rejoice (Phil. 1:15-18).

If, for a while, you have been involved in leading people to
Christ, then you will realize that sometimes people find genuine new life in Christ through "witnesses" who are rather
strange people. The fact that soul-winners can have some
rather obvious sins in their lives indeed is puzzling. But the
gospel itself is the power of God for salvation. In this we also
rejoice. God will use us before we are perfect. Other than
Jesus Himself, no one serves God perfectly. God's grace is
amazing. And aren't we all glad for that? The sovereign will of
God, expressed through His grace, sometimes allows us to be
at the right place at the right time. We cannot plan for that,
even though we do best by cooperating when we can.

The second variable that determines the extent of our harvest is our faithfulness to what God has said. When we obey,
He rewards us. This is why, on purpose, we try. God tells us to
go, so we go. God tells us to share our faith in Christ, so we
share our faith in Christ. We want to please God as best we
can. We believe that obeying our King will expand the
Kingdom. We believe that a direct relationship exists between
our faithfulness and His blessings. God gives us rewards for
our faithfulness by grace. God gives us gifts, apart from our
efforts, by grace. Gifts and rewards are by grace. This is not an
either/or issue; it is a both/and issue. Rewards are biblical. The
on-purpose trying with your mind and will are biblical.
Choosing to obey is biblical.

Apart from Him we can do nothing, so we want to be with
Him—doing what He wants done. Do we not go into great

detail, and with great effort, to preach that Jesus is Lord? Let us remember His Great Commandment with great detail and great effort. I note that we are to proclaim Jesus as Savior with great detail and great effort. Should we not proclaim Jesus as Lord with great detail and great effort? If we do not proclaim the Lord's Great Commandment, on which rests "*all the Law and the Prophets*", with great effort and detail, then we are not proclaiming what the Lord commands.

Rulers have rules. Commanders have commands. Masters insist that their servants obey the master's own priorities.

> "*Does the Lord delight in burnt offerings and sacrifices as much as in obeying the voice of the Lord? To obey is better than sacrifice, and to heed is better than the fat of rams. For rebellion is like the sin of divination, and arrogance like the evil of idolatry. Because you have rejected the word of the Lord, he has rejected you*" (1 Sam. 15:22-23).

We all prefer to see ourselves as those who preach Christ out of goodwill. Yet the Scripture says that those who preach Christ out of goodwill do so in love. God has defined for us what such love is. On purpose the love of God is accomplished and enables us to be pleasing somebodies who gain much. Love is the most excellent way.

To succeed, all of our programs require intentional planning. We put the most emphasis on the parts of the plan that are most important. Always place the most emphasis on loving God and our brothers and sisters in Christ and on the lost we seek to reach. How many times have our plans been sabotaged by unloving participants? How many annoying nobodies that gain nothing are required to give the devil a foothold? How many lost people have been offended by unloving words and deeds in the midst of our efforts to give them new life in Christ? How many babes in Christ have left your church, in part, because someone sinned against them by being less than loving? How many young Christian leaders have been pummeled into thinking that programs and plans never work, without realizing that the failure was assured when love was ignored or taken for granted? Programs and plans are not sin; the failure to love is sin. Love is not granted; it is purposely done.

How clearly do our preachers and teachers proclaim precisely what love is so that the congregation can discern the difference between the annoying nobodies who gain nothing and the pleasant somebodies who gain much? If the light of God's Word shines brightly on public sin, then the sinners repent or flee. If, in a sincere congregation, the love of God is sincerely and repeatedly defined and emphasized as the Great Commandment, those who are unloving in word and deed will find maintaining influence to be difficult.

How many of our myriad programs and plans have the love of God written into them? The fact is that American Christians are confused about the concept of love; yet on-purpose loving can become self-evident to us. As a whole we do not do it very well. Can it be said of us, in the context of the last days, *Because of the increase of wickedness, the love of most will grow cold*" (Matt. 24:12)?

The fact that the American church is making a tremendous impact on the world through missions efforts is obvious. Might this be the sovereign will of God, expressed through grace? Because we believe the plain-sense meaning of God's words, we are doing some things right. Even if we do not emphasize the love of God definitively, at least we are loving God indirectly, occasionally, and incidentally. What might God do if we made the Great Commandment our great priority? Is loving

God indirectly, occasionally, and incidentally adequate? Dare we risk satisfaction with anything less than loving God with all of our hearts, all of our souls, all of our minds, and all of our strength?

To the harvest! Use a program. Plan carefully. If the programs and plans did not work, they never would become popular. They are popular because they work. Any plan is better than no plan at all. In a spiritual sense they work by the grace and blessing of our Sovereign Creator. Grace alone is wonderful. Grace and the rewards of blessing are even better. Seek the best; the glory of Jesus Christ deserves it.

The gospel is good news

We are to go into all the world and make disciples of every nation. Certainly this begins when God converts an unbeliever into a believer. When the lost person realizes that he or she is sinful, that person seeks a Savior. Jesus Christ certainly saves us from the penalty of our sins through His blood, shed on the cross. Because He is the infinite God who became a human being, He is able to pay our infinite penalty, for sin is infinitely evil. By His resurrection we know that He is alive. All authority in heaven and earth has been given to Him. Jesus Christ is our living Lord, our King. His kingdom never will end.

I forever will be grateful for what He has done for me. Without Him I would be in hell forever (probably already). I also forever will be grateful for what He does for me every single day. He is an active God who continually works in the lives of His children. The gospel is good news. The good news is much, much more than just a rescue from wrath. Wrath refers to punishment and death. The gospel refers to life and peace. Yet wrath, punishment, suffering, and eternal torment are truth and have their place.

By the fear of the Lord we persuade others. The fear of the Lord is an eternal virtue. Even the holy angels, who do not sin, fear God greatly. The fear of the Lord is the beginning both of understanding and of wisdom. But the good news is more than the fear of the Lord. We are called to eternal life—to the abundant life.

Eternal life is more than eternal existence; people in the lake of fire will have eternal existence. Eternal life is more than looking backward in time to what Christ did on the cross. From our created point of view God's eternal purpose for redeemed humankind is in the present and the future, not the past. Eternal life is lived forward.

> *"For you granted him (Jesus) authority over all people that he might give eternal life to all those you have given him. Now this is eternal life: that they may know you, the only true God, and Jesus Christ whom you have sent"* (John 17:2-3).

Eternal life is knowing the Father and the Son. Certainly the Holy Spirit, who is our Counselor, Teacher, and Guide will teach us about God. In doing so He will teach us about Himself, for He also is God. The way He teaches us about righteousness and judgment always is loving. No need exists for us to teach God about us. As the Holy Spirit teaches us about God, He will include what God wants from us and what God wants for us. God is love (1 John 4:8,16). The infinite God is more than love, but He never is less than love. The fact that we can convince ourselves that we want to know God, who is spirit, and yet we may not want to know what the love of God is, which is spiritual, is a curious thing.

99

Can we, on purpose, know God? Is getting to know God something that just happens to us? Is our role in knowing God entirely passive?

If knowing God is something that we, on purpose, cannot try to do, then what is the point of obedience? What is the point of thinking? What is the point of trying?

Love is the most excellent way. God may call a billion people to a billion different walks of life, but the "way we walk" is what matters more than does the mileage we cover. The ends do not justify the means; the means are the end.

The man who says, "I know him," but does not do
what he commands is a liar, and the truth is not in him.
But if anyone obeys his word, God's love is truly made
complete in him. This is how we know we are in him:
Whoever claims to live in him must walk as Jesus did
(1 John 2:4-6).

The gospel—the good news—is salvation from sin and the direction and ability to walk in love. Eternal life is more than love, but it never is less than love. The good news is about salvation from the misery and decay of sin and about the joy and wholesomeness of righteousness.

God made him who had no sin to be sin for us, so that
in him we might become the righteousness of God
(2 Cor. 5:21).

Are you becoming the righteousness of God? Is this what you have become? Most Christians are not focused on being what God wants them to be in this world. Most often we interpret the above passage to speak of the distant future and to be something unobtainable in this world. Our lives demand such

100

an honest conclusion, because our experience in this world does not measure up to the weight of the moral teaching in the Bible. Yet if we consciously focused on the Great Commandment, we would fulfill all the Law and the Prophets. The gospel is good news, because we can, on purpose, live the Great Commandment. It gives life to all those nourished by it.

New life in Jesus Christ is being pure and sinless in the sight of God. But He doesn't make us pure and sinless so that He can set us on a shelf and admire us. We are not some sort of collection! We are God's workmanship, created in Christ Jesus to do good works, which He has prepared in advance for us to do. So, on purpose, do them lovingly, so that you are a pleasant somebody who gains something.

People do not always have a difficult time realizing that sin is real and that it destroys their lives. Miserable people know what sin does. Miserable people need to know and see what the love of God does. Sometimes they need to know that eternal life is the best way to live. This is part of the gospel, too.

Disciples are taught to obey

The Great Commission is to make disciples who will obey what Jesus has commanded. That begins with the Great Commandment, also known as the New Commandment (John 13:34), the Law of Christ (Gal. 6:2), and the Royal Law found in Scripture (Jas. 2:8).

The Great Commission is to make disciples who will obey what Jesus has commanded. The command to love God, our neighbor, and even our enemies fulfills the Law of God that Moses gave. The Law through Moses was intended to make us aware of sin and never was intended to impart life. The Law of Moses kills. Yet through Christ and the New Covenant, once

God has made us alive with Christ, on purpose we live that eternal life, with the love of God as our first and intentional priority. God is highly motivated to empower you to live a life of love. Jesus does not leave you nor forsake you; He is with you until the very end of the age. And He has told us He wants to work shoulder to shoulder with us. He is working shoulder to shoulder with us. He wants you to recognize the truth and to be free to try with optimism, hope, satisfaction, and success.

"Come to me, all you who are weary and burdened, and I will give you rest. Take my yoke upon you and learn from me, for I am gentle and humble in heart, and you will find rest for your souls. For my yoke is easy, and my burden is light" (Matt. 11:28-30).

On purpose, disciples learn. They are active, not just passive. Disciples try. Disciples think. True disciples love God, their neighbors, and even their enemies with all of their hearts and all of their souls and all of their minds and all of their strength. True disciples are known because they love each other. Real Christians are all around you. Do you recognize them?

You cannot know them if you think the love of God is some indefinable mixture of infatuation, romance, preference, physical intimacy, and friendship. Try the spirits to see if they are of God. Try yourself first. Be a disciple.

Chapter 10

The Love of God
and Discipleship

"A new command I give you: Love one another. As I have loved you, so you must love one another. By this will all men know that you are my disciples, if you love one another" *(John 13:34-35).*

Disciples are people who want to become like their teacher. They are so committed to becoming like their teacher that they, on purpose, learn and begin doing what they learn. Disciples develop habits of learning and doing. Disciples begin doing what they learn and do not stop when they make mistakes. Disciples want to become like their teachers and not merely to "study" their teachers. Disciples want to become like their teachers and not just "know" what their teachers "know". Disciples follow a master's direction about what is most important.

Disciples of Jesus Christ want to be like Jesus now, in this world. They have an absolute commitment to learning and then obeying. They have been given, and they cooperate with, the precious gift of repentance. They want Jesus Christ to indwell them in the very heart of their beings. They worship Jesus Christ. They desire to be like Him by learning what He teaches and then by doing it.

Disciples of Jesus Christ intentionally love God and their neighbors with all of their hearts, souls, minds, and strength. This is their Master's commandment, so this is their life's ambition. To one of His disciples, Jesus' saying, "By this will all men know that you are my disciples, if you love one another", is not a surprising identifying mark. According to God Himself, this is how we know who the true disciples of Jesus Christ are. This is the normal description, and not an idealized one, of a disciple. We attain it with our purposeful intent. In the process we are active and not passive.

A person purposely becomes a disciple of Jesus. If I do not conform to the Lord's definition of "His disciple", then I am not "His disciple". What kind of arrogance must I possess if I prefer to change His definition of *disciple*, rather than preferring to change myself? Why would I prefer not changing myself? I want to be like Him; I do not want to pretend He is like me. He who has eyes to see, let Him see.

At Antioch the disciples first were called *Christians* (Acts 11:26b). Men and women who wanted to learn about Jesus Christ so they could do what Jesus did (John 14:12) first were called *Christians* because they were like the Christ. The logical case certainly can be made that the terms *disciple* and *Christian* essentially are the same. How can we conclude that God is pleased with us if we believe that we are a "Christian" without being a "disciple"?

As a constant reminder, disciples are not infatuated with each other, they are not romantically inclined toward each other, they are not physically intimate with each other. Instead, they love each other God's way, so He makes the disciple's relationships holy. According to God's definition of *love* they, on purpose, love each other. They intentionally choose the most excellent way. Disciples are pleasant somebodies who gain much and are not annoying nobodies who gain nothing.

Discipleship training

Are American Christians "Christian" if they are not disciples? If they are not, this is not for lack of enough fine discipleship plans. A disciple can follow Billy Hanks and Dawson Trotman. The disciple can use fine materials by Henry Blackaby (*Experiencing God*) and/or Avery Willis (*MasterLife*). Mature disciples will pick and choose from the advice of these Christian mentors and develop their own effective biblical disciplines.

As the years go by, mature disciples will love God and others better and better, even if they are loving God's way indirectly, occasionally, and incidentally. A couple of decades of my life are invested in this indirect, occasional, and incidental way. But a better way is to love intentionally. Love rationally. On purpose, love with your mind. In loving God and others with an intentional focus you will be a better steward of your opportunities. You will redeem the time. You will be a pleasing somebody who gains much.

We have four ways to categorize common components of discipleship. Let's apply the Great Commandment to these four ways: Bible study, prayer, membership, and witness.

The disciple and the Bible

When we, as Americans, discuss truth, remember that we live in a relative society. The vast majority of Americans, in church and out, live as if truth is relative to the point of view of each individual. From the American point of view, I agree with them.

Truth is relative. What is true for me might not be true for you. Fine. What is true for you might not be true for me. That also is fine; we all are entitled to our own opinions. Now, let's give the infinite Creator God the dignity that we are willing to give to other people. What's true for you might not be true for God. And what is true for God might not be true for you. That raises a massive problem. God says He will hold you responsible for what you believe and do. You cannot hold Him responsible in the same way. He is the infinite God and will do what He wants. Who can tell Him "No!" when He decides to judge?

The infinite God understands, from an infinite point of view, all of creation and history. He absolutely understands you and everything else. God actually believes He is God. He is not affected by moral peer-pressure, for He has no peers. He is not affected by majority opinion. By definition an infinite God can think through everything every second. That makes His opinions absolute truth. This is the God Who, in Jesus Christ, became a human being. Here's what He says about truth:

> *"But whoever lives by the truth comes into the light, so that it may be seen plainly that what he has done has been done through God"* (John 3:21).

In this passage *truth* and *light* are synonymous. If the words are reversed, the passage essentially means the same thing. "*Whoever lives by the light comes into the truth, so that it may be seen plainly that what he has done has been done through God.*" God is the One who defines the truth of reality, regardless of human opinion or sincerity. The truth of God, like light, defines what we have done and makes it visible. The disciple of Jesus Christ will emerge into the light—the truth, as God desires.

> *To the Jews who had believed him, Jesus said, "If you hold to my teaching, you are really my disciples. Then*

you will know the truth, and the truth will set you free"
(John 8:31-32).

Here, along with many other passages, Jesus relates His teaching—His words—as the truth. He is not just referring to the sincerity of His intent to be honest. His teaching is the absolutely accurate opinion of God. Jesus' teaching is the inerrant representation of reality according to God. Part of God's gracious intent for our growth is that knowing the truth is central to how He changes us. The truth of God sets us free of sin. The truth of God changes us. Knowing the truth is spiritual interaction. Obeying the truth is spiritual interaction. To be a disciple of Jesus, the living Word of God (John 1:1-14), is to be a disciple of His teaching.

> *Jesus answered, "I am the way and the truth and the life. No one comes to the Father except through me"* (John 14:6).

Here Jesus speaks in a singular fashion of "the truth". One Truth exists. Jesus is the Truth. As the Word of God, Jesus is the expression of the belief and desire of God, just as our words express our beliefs and desires. He is the infinite Creator God Who also became a human being. To be His disciple is to conform your beliefs and your actions to His will. You have no way to approach God without going through Jesus Christ, who is the living Word of God; He is the Truth.

Jesus Christ is the living Word. The fact that the infinite God is more than the finite Bible is obvious. But the Bible, literally, is the Word of God. The Word of God changes us. Jesus Christ changes us. Both are in harmony, because they are one. Jesus Christ is more than the Bible, but He never is less, nor contrary to, the Bible.

As Jesus prayed to the Father, He said,

"Sanctify them by the truth; your word is truth"
(John 17:17).

To *sanctify* means to "make holy"—to "set above". To sanctify someone is to change that person. The one sanctified is passive, while the change agent is active. The Truth, the Word of God, is the active change agent. That is Who Jesus is before He became a human being. In the world, the Word of God (the change agent) interacts with disciples to make them more like their teacher, Jesus Christ. The Word of God is at work in those who believe God. The Apostle Paul said to the Thessalonian disciples:

"And we also thank God continually because, when you received the word of God, which you heard from us, you accepted it not as the word of men, but as it actually is, the word of God, which is at work in you who believe" (1 Thess. 2:13).

When the Word of God is planted in a sincere seeker-after-God, It changes the individual. The Word of God never returns to Him empty. It always accomplishes God's desire and achieves the purpose for which God sent It (Isa. 55:10-11). When the Word of God is planted in a sincere disciple of Jesus Christ, and that disciple will do what It says (Jas. 1:22), It always brings about the righteous life that God desires.

Therefore, get rid of all moral filth and the evil that is so prevalent and humbly accept the word planted in you, which can save you (Jas. 1:21).

This passage was written to those who already were born-again worshipers of Jesus Christ. Those for whom this message was intended already were serious about being disciples of Jesus Christ. The passage is not talking about being saved from wrath but being saved from moral filth and the evil that is so prevalent. The Word of God that is planted in you can save you from present sin—from current vice.

These are some of the reasons why Bible study is so important. *"Man does not live on bread alone, but on every word that comes from the mouth of God"* (Matt. 4:4). One cannot exaggerate the futility and absurdity of pretending to love Jesus Christ without an equivalent love of His Word. The desire to be like Jesus has no integrity if we have no identical, sincere desire to hear, remember, and obey His words.

How can (or will) disciples possibly not remember (memorize) the words of their master? The Word of God forever is true and forever is powerful. A multitude of times during their lives the same passage empowers the disciples. Disciples will hide in their hearts the Word of God (Ps. 199:11). Disciples will produce abundant spiritual virtue (Matt. 13:34). Disciples will stand on a foundation that cannot be undermined (Matt. 7:24-27). God has ordained that His words are necessary components to our faith (Rom. 10:17). The advantages of memorizing and doing what God says literally are endless.

If you can understand language, then you can remember what is important to you. You do it all the time. Remembering the words is necessary to understand language. If you can remember the words of a whole language, then you can memorize Scripture. If you cannot memorize Scripture, then doing so is not important to you. If this statement makes you angry, then you are able to remember this statement. Perhaps remembering that you have guilt because you do not memorize Scripture is important to you. Why do you remember the guilt instead of the Scripture? You obviously can remember, so why not remember how God says to eliminate guilt? As a Christian, you do not have to live with guilt.

We have a most excellent way to memorize and do what God says. Begin with what is most important. Memorize the Great Commandment (Matt. 22:37-40) and God's clear definition of what *love* is (1 Cor. 13:4-8a). Now apply it to all your words, all your thinking, and all your actions (1 Cor.13:1-3). This will help the new Christian grow stronger faster. This will reinvigorate the discouraged Christian, because for the first time in his or her life, the person is directly doing what God wants done. Only this way can your love abound so that you can discern what is best (Phil. 1:9-10).

Disciples of Jesus Christ will discipline themselves to do what Jesus says is most important. In this world this is the only way to be like Him.

The disciple and prayer

Prayer is talking to God. You and God both are people. He is the big Person; you are the little one. As with all conversations between people, we listen as well as speak. God's communication to you is most clear and reliable when you are reading the Bible. While you read the Bible, you obviously can respond to what God is saying. God tells us to pray without ceasing. This is like talking to another person when the person is present. You talk some; you listen some. You respond to each other's thoughts and desires. While a time for formal prayer—all alone, on your knees—certainly exists, to pray without ceasing is to treat God as if He were present and communicating with you. Even Jesus did not spend 100 percent of His time on His knees! Talking to God and listening for His response is no more of a burden than is having a conversation with any other infinitely wise, infinitely loving, and infinitely interesting person you may know.

On occasion, the maturity of two people who are talking will be unequal. A toddler can have a talk with Grandpa. A talk between God and people can occur the same way. New believers pray like infants talk. Their requests are simple. I want a hug. I'm hungry. I don't feel good. All of these requests are reasonable. In this world they never become unreasonable. Sometimes Grandpa wants a hug, or is hungry, or doesn't feel good. God cares about all of these requests. He gives us the insights and creativity we need at the level of maturity in which we dwell.

These simple and necessary prayer requests are kind-of like general housekeeping. As long as you live in the house, certain things need to be done to keep the house clean and in good repair. We always will need hugs and food and comfort. God knows what we need, but He does not want us to live for hugs, food, and comfort.

> *"For the pagans run after all these things, and your heavenly Father knows that you need them. But seek first his kingdom and his righteousness, and all these things will be given to you as well"* (Matt. 6:32-33).

At some point a babe in Christ will begin to realize a kingdom is out there to seek and a righteousness is out there to live. All kingdoms are defined by the commands of their kings. Our King, Jesus Christ, has let us know what His Great Commandment is. A disciple willingly will embrace his or her King's command. The righteousness of any kingdom is defined by the king. Jesus Christ has made it clear what the right thing is to do. As we seek His kingdom and His righteousness, all that we need concerning housekeeping prayers will be provided. Of course we still can pray about them. Of course we should remain grateful for them and express our thanks to God. But at some point we grow beyond seeking after them as the pagans do. At some point we grow beyond seeking after them as Christian infants do. We always may pray for health, wealth, comfort, and convenience; just do not stop there.

One possibly can ask, in a sinful manner, for health, wealth, comfort, and convenience. When we ask for something so that we can spend it on our own pleasures, we ask with wrong motives. We will not receive God's approval (Jas. 4:3). God's Great Commandment includes the truth that "love is not self-seeking". For the mature disciple, the majority of prayer always will be for others. The majority of the mature disciple's prayers for himself or herself still will be directed toward the good of others. Whether we are praying for the health and comfort of others, or whether we are praying for someone to receive the precious gift of repentance, the prayers are for the good of others. When the disciple prays for himself or herself, he or she asks that the love of God may abound through him or her more and more (Phil. 1:9-11). As the disciple asks for the specific attributes of the love of God that he or she needs, the disciple knows that the granting of the request will be for the good of others. When I ask for patience, this is so I will be patient with others. When I ask for kindness, this is so that I can be kind to others. As we ask for the love of God, we ask that we can treat others as Jesus Christ does. This is inherently unselfish. God intends that this be normal.

Since the love of God is a choice, and we can be tempted to choose sin, we find we need to ask more directly for some of the attributes of the love of God. Since love is not rude, if I am habitually rude, then I can pray that God will grant me the tact to be polite. Since love always trusts, if I do not know how to build trust, I can talk this over with God, my Maker. He will show me how to build trust. This is the birthright of the Christian.

Jesus Christ wants us to be pleasant somebodies who gain much. This only will happen when we choose to do what He says is absolutely most important. I thank God that I was (at least) indirectly, occasionally, and incidentally a pleasant somebody who gained a little during the first 10 years of my Christian life. Disciples learn what the Master wants; then they remember it and do it. With practice, they get better and better at it. As disciples become more trustworthy, the Master gives them greater opportunities. The more the disciple lives the life of loving others, the more of a blessing he or she is to others. The more you give, the more you can have to give away. This is mature Christian spirituality and always has been so. This always has been true of what God considers to be real treasure.

The world considers other things to be treasure. The world measures treasure according to wealth, fame, and power. The world wants wealth that is measured as health, comfort, and convenience. Now while many famous Bible characters truly accumulated wealth, power, and fame, those who did so because they (on purpose) were after wealth, power, and fame are the villains. God considers them sinful and wicked. Those who are heroes of the faith are those who did what God said to do regardless of whether they would get money, comfort, or convenience. The heroes of the faith led awesome lives of adventure, but they neither were comfortable nor convenient lives. On occasion, when God saw fit to give them material wealth, health, and comfort, the faithful always were unselfish with it. When God said so, they would sacrifice it (even their health). No comfortable and convenient life exists on this sinful planet. We may have comfortable and convenient times, but the only comfortable and convenient mortal life is a pretend life wrapped up in comfortable and convenient lies. The lies feel real good until they betray you. And these lies, and those who believe them, soon will be consumed in the lake of fire.

How much better to be a disciple who actually values, above all things, the love of God! How much better to be one who accurately can ask for what God actually wants to give!

> *"I tell you the truth, anyone who has faith in me will do what I have been doing. He will do even greater things than these, because I am going to the Father. And I will do whatever you ask in my name, so that the Son may bring glory to the Father. You may ask me for anything in my name, and I will do it"* (John 14:12-14).

Certainly a relationship exists between spiritual maturity and the accuracy of praying according to God's will. Mature Christians spend most of their time cooperating with the Father's greatest priorities. On purpose choose to love God and others. All of your past intentions that are indirect, occasional, and incidental are remembered. They are the parts of your life for which you will be rewarded.

Now choose to obey the Great Commandment with all of your heart, all of your soul, all of your strength, and all of your mind. Upgrade all indirect, occasional, and incidental discipleship to an intentional focus. Upgrade all indirect, occasional, and incidental growth to an intentional focus. The upgrades always are free; they never fail you. Choose to grow at the maximum pace God will allow by choosing to cooperate with God's maximum priority. We have no better plan. He already has given us the most excellent way.

Discipleship and membership

I have chosen to call this section "Discipleship and membership" to breathe awareness into the biblical concept of being a member of the body of Christ. American Christians might be more familiar with this idea if we phrase it *service*, *ministry*, or *good works*. Regardless of how one prefers to think of Christian activity, the disciple is to be involved in activity. Disciples want to be like Jesus in this world, not merely aware of what Jesus did and does.

Now you are the body of Christ, and each of you is a part of it (1 Cor. 12:27).

But in fact God has arranged the parts of the body, every one of them, just as he wanted them to be (1 Cor. 12:18).

The body is a unit, though it is made up of many parts; and though all its parts are many, they form one body. So it is with Christ (1 Cor. 12:12).

Now to each one the manifestation of the Spirit is given for the common good (1 Cor. 12:7).

God the Father, God the Son, and God the Spirit are one. They have the same moral values and the same priority for those values. They all agree, without compromise, that their Great Commandment is their great priority. The body of Christ, which is the church, is to reflect this.

The word *church* is a translation of the Greek word *ecclesia*, which means "called-out ones". God calls people to new life in Christ. He does not call us to emerge from the world and be passive and inactive. He calls us to purposeful activity. We see this in 1 Corinthians 12. To have a healthy body, active body parts are necessary. People are the parts of the body of Christ. To be active they must decide what to do. The parts of the body that are not active include parts such as fat and tumors. They consume oxygen and nutrients but do not directly contribute to the overall health of the body.

So what are the parts of the body supposed to do? Even "Christians" who do not believe the plain-sense meaning of Scripture know that we are to feed the poor, visit and nourish the sick, visit those who are in jail, and clothe the naked. Non-Christian religions also know and practice these things. Within the body of Christ and in the world, by sharing the gospel we also are to make disciples and glorify God.

On purpose, you do all of these activities. You never have done one of these things without thinking about it. How is that better than the pagans? They do most of these things, too. The Christian distinctive is that all of these things are done with the love of God foremost in our plans. We feed the poor lovingly; then the Holy Spirit empowers our efforts. The Holy Spirit allows us to cooperate with Him when we, in the love of God, visit those who are in prison. As we share the gospel with the lost, they can see that Jesus is alive because His body is loving them at the point at which they are. The "*manifestation of the Spirit is given for the common good.*" Christians who are annoying nobodies who gain nothing are common, but they are not good.

In our pluralistic society a poor, sick, or imprisoned person may receive help, be nourished to health, or be visited by people with a wide variety of religious preferences. What will stand out to this peron? Those who love them God's way.

While Jesus Christ obviously miraculously met the physical needs of those who needed ministry, we can see in the gospels that Jesus met those needs lovingly. While Jesus worked awesome miracles to demonstrate that He was the infinite Creator, and the apostles worked awesome miracles to demonstrate that they were apostles empowered by the infinite Creator, we are to meet these same physical needs with the supernatural power of the love of God. We are not the Messiah, nor are we His apostles. But we are the body of Christ; we are to be active in the body and do our part.

American Christians on occasion love indirectly. The fact that hearers are transformed into Christlikeness is an incidental result of the Word of God. This is wonderful, but it is better still if we love directly, continually, and with our highest purpose. This is normal for mature believers. Mature believers are immune to the cunning and craftiness of people in their deceitful scheming.

Instead, speaking the truth in love, we will in all things grow up into him who is the Head, that is, Christ. From him the whole body, joined and held together by every supporting ligament, grows and builds itself up in love as each part does its work (Eph. 4:15-16).

I have talked with a great many Christians who are discouraged about getting involved in the local church. They have been hurt. They feed the poor in the company of mean Christians. They visit the sick with impatient Christians. They attend Bible class with rude teachers who destroy trust. They fellowship with "members" of the body of Christ who gossip and lust for power (influence) in the church. They are caught in a fellowship of Christian talkers who do not practice the Great Commandment. Someone who only "talks" Christian but lives worldly is no better than someone who talks and lives worldly. Often this kind of person is worse. The sincere and consistent "worldling" often is more understandable (and pleasant) than is the Christian hypocrite. I actually prefer the company of a lost person to that of a hypocrite. That lost person's words and actions agree more often.

Chapter 11

The Love of God
and the Truth

The love of God is not an emotion. It is not a sensual passion. It is not a feeling, nor are we powerfully moved to love from a nebulous source apart from reason. The love of God is choosing to do what God said is most important. He is most motivated to empower us to do what He considers best. God's definition of *love* can be cooperated with (obeyed), whether or not we feel like it.

While we seek to love God and others, our emotional state affects our perspective. Sometimes we are highly emotional; sometimes we are not. We can be kind with great passionate feeling, or we can be kind because we choose to be so. We can attempt to protect another from a high emotional state in which all of our senses are at an adrenaline-aided peak (sensuality), or we can seek to protect someone from a cool, dispassionate point-of-view. Love is kind; love always protects; so be kind and protect others. Your emotional state while you are doing so is not the major issue with God.

Our emotional state of being is real. The question of whether we are emotionally active is pointless. We always are emotionally active. If your blood is flowing, you are emotional. The practical issue is realizing how emotional you are being at any given time. Our passion and sensuality always are in effect, so how we feel always affects our love of God and others. But the love of God does not flow from our passion and sensuality; it flows from the Holy Spirit by grace through our wills. Sometimes toning down the level of emotion we feel is necessary. Such acts of will are known as self-control. The love of God is effective and does not depend on emotion. The love of God is emotion-neutral.

Except for one, all of the ways God defines *love* are emotion-neutral.

 Love does not delight in evil but rejoices with the truth (1 Cor. 13:6).

Rejoicing is an emotional word. The object of our joy stirs our passion within us. The love of God stirs us to be emotionally involved with the truth. We are to be passionate about the truth. We are to allow the truth to elevate our senses. Ideally the truth stirs your pulse and maintains your attention. We have no need for serious concerns about our personal spirituality if we do not rejoice with the truth.

Again the biblical words for emotion are passion and sensuality. Passion and the senses are God-created and designed to harmonize with virtues such as the truth. That is why God created emotional experience. Emotions have a God-intended purpose. Part of that purpose is to rejoice with the truth.

Truth from the human perspective

Often we consider our remembrance of events, recounted with all personal sincerity, as the same as the truth. We stand plainly for what we saw and heard and for what we said and did. From the human perspective this is accurate. In courts of law we want the witnesses to tell "the truth, the whole truth, and nothing but the truth". Telling the truth builds trust; telling less than the truth destroys trust. Accurately perceiving the truth can be called *sanity*. Accurately communicating the truth can be called *sincerity*.

Sanity and sincerity are universally acclaimed virtues. While the variety of human cultures with their differing moral codes is vast, no society trusts the insane person—even less when people know that the insane individual is insincere.

In a sinful world misreading reality is possible.

Each of us lives from year to year with our own, individual human perspective. God designed us this way and holds us accountable for what we perceive. While an excellent biblical argument can be made that God predetermines every thought and action, we acknowledge that God intended us to have a finite, individual point-of-view. Whether or not everything is predetermined, we are held accountable for what we believe and what we do with that belief. While I know that I am living out God's infinitely detailed plan, I also know that I am to cooperate with His plan as if my decisions make a major difference. I have the faith to do so.

At my best I am sincere. Unfortunately at my best I also can be wrong. My perception about what goes on in the lives of those around me can be wrong. I am capable of being sincerely wrong, so sincerity is not a safeguard. Since I do not know what anyone else in my life is thinking, I always interact with incomplete information. Indeed I am incapable of knowing everything, let alone processing such an infinite amount of information.

Therefore I never have all the pertinent information I need to make a perfect decision. In a very real sense I never "play with a full deck". When you are finished laughing, admit that you don't either.

I have concluded that my human perception of truth is inadequate. I cannot be certain of my perception; therefore all my decisions are suspect. Both reason and passion are real, but in a sinful world they are untrustworthy. I easily can agree with Jeremiah when he says:

The heart is deceitful above all things and beyond cure. Who can understand it? (Jer 17:9).

Since the core of my being (my heart) is deceitful and beyond cure, I am incapable of arriving at any absolute truth. All I can do to rejoice in the truth is to rejoice in my own opinion of the truth, which amounts to just rejoicing in my own opinion. If I rejoice in my own opinion, I am being arrogant. Truly, when an arrogant person rejoices in his or her own opinion, does he or she not become a braggart?

He who trusts in himself is a fool, but he who walks in wisdom is kept safe (Prov. 28:26).

Clearly, my sincere recollection of what others said and did and what I said and did are not entirely reliable. My sincere recollections certainly are preferable to my insincere recollections, which thinking people commonly acknowledge as "trying to tell the truth is better than trying to tell a lie."

Yet, when we are thinking of the love of God and the truth, I am hoping God means something more substantial than rejoicing in my own opinion. I think I need to be delivered from my opinions. Somebody save me from myself!

Jesus answered, "I am the way and the truth and the life. No one comes to the Father except through me" (John 14:6).

Let's go over this again. The infinite Creator God, Who knows everything, Who designed everything in infinite detail,

Who thinks everything through infinitely all the time, became a person in Jesus Christ. I can rejoice in His perception. I can rejoice in His reasoning ability. I can rejoice in His sincerity. I can rejoice in His sanity. He is my Savior from uncertainty as well as my Savior from wrath.

Truth from the divine perspective

God alone is capable of telling "the truth, the whole truth, and nothing but the truth". God's remembrance of events perfectly coincides with His design of the events. Perfectly and infinitely He is aware of the context of the past and the future. God knows why people said what they said and why they did what they did (Heb. 4:12, 13). He knows what they meant, even if they themselves didn't. For a very long time He has known what would happen. God's opinion of "who" said "what" is perfect and worthy of trust. Telling the truth increases trust.

Accurately perceiving the truth is sanity. God is sane. Accurately communicating the truth is sincerity. God is sincere. God's perspective on reality is perfect and wholly trustworthy. What God has said has been proven trustworthy so many thousands of times in my life that I take great comfort in what He says. I rejoice in the truth. What God proclaims gives us certainty, regardless of what any number of humans may say. All of humanity plays with less than a full deck. The consensus of 600 million "perceptually challenged" humans brings me no comfort.

Sanity and sincerity are universally acclaimed virtues. And yet most of the world rejects the truth of God. The rejection of sincere sanity should be cause for concern. Certainly it should weigh heavily on whether or not someone else is truthful from

God's point of view, or only rejoicing, sincerely, in their own opinion. The truth of Christ is Christian truth; people who are not Christian never will accept it (1 Cor. 2:14). They are unable to appreciate divine sanity. Jesus said,

> *"Why is my language not clear to you? Because you*
> *are unable to hear what I say.*
> *Yet because I tell the truth, you do not believe me!"*
> (John 8:43, 45).

Yet love rejoices with the truth. The Great Commandment, the New Commandment, the Law of Christ, require a noticeable joy in what God says. Rejoicing in the words of God may be easy when they agree with your opinions. But when the Word of God conflicts with your preferences, will you admit your preferences are sinful? At the point you refuse to rejoice with the truth, you become the annoying nobody who gains nothing. Disbelieving the word of God is unloving. It is sin. Don't miss this point. By God's own definition of *love,* to refuse to rejoice in the plain-sense meaning of what God has said is unloving.

The truth of God daily reveals my sin. Rejoicing in the presence of habitual guilt sometimes is difficult. How can I ever hope to rejoice in the truth that reveals my sin if I do not admit it is sin? No doubt I have sinful desires. Do I want to overcome them? Denying sin before God is unacceptable to God. Love is not proud; therefore love is humble. And humility begins with the realization and admission of one's own sins.

> *If we claim to be without sin, we deceive ourselves and*
> *the truth is not in us. If we confess our sins, he is*
> *faithful and just and will forgive us our sins and purify*
> *us from all unrighteousness. If we claim we have not*

sinned, we make him out to be a liar and his word has no place in our lives (1 John 1:8-10).

If you want to love God with all your heart, all your soul, all your mind, and all your strength, have the sincere humility to recognize your own sin, call it sin, ask for forgiveness, and seek actual repentance. Merely to stop sinning is not repentance. Repentance is stopping sin and beginning the corresponding virtue. If the Bible makes a moral claim that you do not like, seek to have what you "like" changed to the point that you rejoice that your old desire was sinful. It only seems sincere if your new, repentant desire, is holy. If God shows you the truth, that truth sets you free. If you have the confidence that God wants you to stop sinning and to live lovingly, then seek the love of God. Seek the love of God as if everything depends on it, because it does. And love rejoices with the truth.

> *Love does not delight in evil, but rejoices with the truth* (1 Cor. 13:6).

Now compare this passage with the following passage. Note the similarities about the delight in evil and the love of the truth.

> *They perish because they refused to love the truth and so be saved. For this reason, God sends them a powerful delusion so that they will believe the lie and so that all will be condemned who have not believed the truth but have delighted in wickedness* (2 Thess. 2:10b-12).

Love rejoices with the truth. Love does not just tolerate the truth. Love rejoices with the truth even if 600 million people disagree about what the truth is. Tolerance for the truth of the Bible is unacceptable. People perish because they refuse to love the truth. A passion for rejoicing in the truth is necessary to survive powerful delusions. Examples of contemporary failure are more numerous than are examples of contemporary success.

What happens when a denomination of the Christian tradition finds the statements of the Bible "out-of-step" with competing contemporary moral codes? What happens when the Word of God through the apostles and prophets enters into conflict with the moral priorities of the courts or the universities or legislation passed by the perceptually challenged majority of the citizens in a sinful world?

A Christian denomination, if it is to stay Christian, will rejoice in the truth. Passion for the truth will surface and will be noticeable. Faithful Christians of a denomination in crisis publicly will love the truth and enter into increasingly public conflict with those who refuse to love the truth. Those who refuse publicly to love the truth are the ones who are delighting in evil. Is making such a sweeping statement accurate? I make the statement because I believe that "evil" and "wickedness" essentially are the same thing. I also think that disagreeing with God in order to agree with the politicians and professors is ungodly. What do you think?

The wrath of God is being revealed from heaven against all the godlessness and wickedness of men who suppress the truth by their wickedness (Rom. 1:18).

Have you noticed the suppression of Christian truth? Within the communities of faith, whether Old Testament or New Testament or since the completion of the New Testament, this conflict is constant. Virtually every book of the Bible is, in

126

part, a record of those who love the truth in conflict with those who try to suppress the truth. According to the above passage, the suppression of truth is wickedness.

The middle ground in such conflicts is asserted by those who try to tolerate the truth. Privately they attempt to work out the "problems" with those who rejoice with the truth. Adherents to this point of view tend to be embarrassed by some of the statements of Scripture. Far from rejoicing in the truth, they are ashamed in public by some of the truth. Such a middle ground really is no middle ground at all. Jesus said,

> "*If anyone is ashamed of me and my words, the Son of Man will be ashamed of him . . .* " (Luke 9:26a).

A common theme among those who suppress the truth in the name of Christ is the moral preference for "kindness, forgiveness, peace, tolerance, and love". But if they do not love the truth of God, then their "love" is not the love of God at all. It cannot be the love of God because,

> *Love does not delight in evil but rejoices with the truth* (1 Cor. 13:6).

If their "love" is not the love of God, then why follow them? If they are suppressing the truth, then why support them? If their influence is unfaithful, then why submit your family to their influence?

I am a Southern Baptist by choice. I was not reared this way. I was not reared as a Christian. Yet, by choice, I am a Christian and a Southern Baptist. The Southern Baptist Convention has been going through such a conflict. State conventions now are going through this conflict. Local associations and local churches still are going through this conflict. I am not surprised; this is nothing new. Trials of faith, both personal and corporate, are the rule and not the exception on this planet. Trials of faith, both personal and corporate, are the rule in the Bible. This is a sinful world, remember? Read the Word of God. Get a solid dose of divine sanity.

I like the Southern Baptist conservative-resurgence movement, though I think it is better called "biblical repentance". I actually am impressed that a religious organization that is several generations old actually has reversed a slide into unfaithfulness. In the Bible or church history I cannot find a similar precedent. This is a very, very rare blessing. I hope that our future love of each other may be by intentional focus. If the grace of God that follows indirect, occasional, and incidental obedience to the Great Commandment is blessing without precedent, what might an intentional focus on God's great priority bring?

I like the Southern Baptist biblical repentance. I hope it continues and does not die of apathy. Shall we really say to our King, Jesus Christ, "Hey! We are faithful enough! No more of this conflict stuff." Or would you prefer, "But Master! We have arrived! We are the most splendid people ever to live on your planet!"

In the young moral timidity is tolerated for a while. But when moral timidity grows up, it really is moral cowardice. I agree that an unloving conflict over truth is annoying and that the unloving participants in such a conflict are nobodies who gain nothing. But not everyone is unloving. Do not deny the spiritual battle because you are unarmed. Do not give aid and comfort to those who suppress the truth because it causes you discomfort. Rise to the occasion. Set the example of how, in moral conflicts, people can be like Jesus.

Chapter 12

The Love of God
and Personal Confrontation

Most personal conflicts involve sin. In America we commonly consider such sinful confrontations as mere "personality conflicts". When two people cannot seem to find a way to get along pleasantly, Americans merely say that the two have personalities that are unable to associate together. Seemingly no moral judgment is warranted. They have "inherent" personality traits that just cannot coexist without conflict.

This may be wonderful pop psychology, but it is not Christianity. We are responsible for the traits of our personality. A personality consists of the repeated traits of a person. A personality is a person's habitual expression of attitude and meaning. The expressions of people either are sinful, or they are not. When I sin, my personality is sinning. When I am sanctified into virtuous personality habits, then this person is virtuous.

However, no matter how far we have traveled in our Christian pilgrimage, in this world we still have problems with personal sin and with encountering the sins of others.

Without any doubt, the preferable way to deal with our discovery of someone else's sin is to cover it with the love of God.

Above all, love each other deeply, because love covers over a multitude of sins (1 Pet. 4:8).

When you attempt to build trust in the presence of a gossip or display the love of God by refusing to be easily angered in the presence of one who is venting, you are giving a living testimony of how to cope faithfully with life's temptations. Remember that the Holy Spirit is moving within all of the people involved. He is far better at convicting others of sin than we are. He is the One who understands the context of the lives that are involved. You are not alone in your conflict. Since God also is involved, you are not even the primary person involved. Our Christian lives ideally are characterized by listening to the other person and enduring their endurable sins until we know how to encourage them. I doubt that a single person on the planet exists who would want us to point out every sin he or she commits every time the person does so.

The on-purpose practicing of this restraint is worthwhile. Every one of your public days will provide you with ample opportunities to cover over the sins of others with your intentional focus on the love of God. Freely display the love of God. The public display of patience, kindness, humility, and unselfishness have a sanctifying effect independent of your goals and motives. A word exists for those who try to confront every individual sin of every person they meet. That word is *lonely.* The purpose of the law is to convict the world of sin; the law kills. So do you if the law is your primary guide in life. You can be part of the solution to any problem you encounter. You cannot be part of the solution to every problem you encounter.

How do you know when to cover a sin with love and when to confront a sin lovingly? In this let your conscience be your guide. In His time the Holy Spirit will give you the wisdom that emerges from experience. If you want to intervene in a life and confront sin, then do so lovingly. If you conclude that doing so is not your business, then do so faithfully. The fact of the matter is that the whole time you are on the planet, God will have you involved with other people and their sins.

Almost every time you try to help another person with his or her sin, you will feel the temptation to anxiety. If you never choose to do what God says to do because you are afraid of anxiety, then that is moral timidity. Anxiety is fear. To be afraid of fear is an advanced form of unfaithfulness. Face your fear faithfully; you will become courageous. Flee from your fear; you reinforce the habit of unfaithfulness.

All disappointment springs from failed expectations. We look forward to a good day but receive a difficult one instead. We prepare for every contingency as we expect a difficult day and are blindsided by a word or event that we could not have foreseen. We look forward to the manifestation of our "pet sin", only to have it fall short of our expectation. Sometimes we sin for no understandable reason. Life on this sinful planet can be disappointing; our sinful response can be a burden to ourselves and to those around us. The love of God compels us and enables us to bear each other's burdens.

> *Brothers, if someone is caught in a sin, you who are spiritual should restore him gently. But watch yourself, or you also may be tempted. Carry each other's burdens, and in this way you will fulfill the law of Christ* (Gal. 6:1-2).

This law of Christ is none other than the Great Commandment. Love is not self-seeking. Love is concerned about the other person. We can help carry another's burden of sin by, on purpose, loving that person. Love is patient and kind. Patience and kindness, when combined, are the definition of gentleness. Once the fear-and-courage issue is settled faithfully, we are ready to restore our brother. Make the restoration gentle.

Take a moment and consider the nature of "restoration". To who or what is the sinning brother to be restored? To you and/or to the church? Perhaps so, but these are secondary considerations. The primary consideration is that the person be restored to fellowship with God. In order to sin, the person is quenching the Spirit. The person is choosing to sin instead of being led by the Spirit. The primary restoration is between the sinning individual and God.

Know for certain that God insists on being involved. Restoration requires that the relationship between the person and Jesus Christ already is a new-covenant relationship. The sinning individual is a born-again Christian. Encourage the sinning person to repent of rebellion against Jesus, the King. Encourage the person to love Jesus Christ with all of his or her heart, soul, mind, and strength. The primary problem with sin is that the sinning Christian is not loving his or her Creator. The sinning Christian is interrupting the relationship between himself or herself and the Holy Spirit of God. What the sinning Christian is doing to other people actually is secondary.

How can I influence a sinning Christian to "want to" repent? I cannot! I have no direct connection to the "will" of the sinning Christian. However, God does have such a direct connection. In an effort to restore one who is caught in a sin, I am not the primary person involved. God is the primary person involved. God has made His strategy extremely clear.

We have a Great Commandment. To the extent that we intentionally focus on what God wants to do, we intentionally focus on what God actually is doing in the restoration relationship. This is intensely practical. When we are attempting to influence someone's behavior in a way that is not intentionally focused on what God wants to do, then we are not being helpful; we are getting in the way. We actually become a distraction. This is understandable. Cooperating with God is a skill that He is highly motivated to teach us. It is the most excellent way.

The best way to restore an individual is to have the person immediately transported into the very presence of Jesus Christ Himself! I have had no success whatsoever with this method. The next best way is to have angels supernaturally confront the sinning individual with the holiness of God. I continually have failed with this plan, also. However, if I take a loving attitude into the relationship with the sinning man or woman and lovingly speak the truth of God to the person (quick to listen, slow to speak), then this sinning individual receives the ministry of the Word of God through the love of God, from within the image of God (humanity). God is love. By grace, you are the body of Christ speaking the words of God in the love of God. In a New Covenant sense this is a supernatural occurrence. It occurs as often as you want it to happen. It is your birthright. Sorry; this is not accompanied by any flash-and-bang soundtracks or shock-and-awe emotional manifestations. Why not participate in what God actually is doing instead of holding out for (or pretending to) better terms?

When the sinning person is restored to right relationship with Jesus Christ, then all the other damaged relationships can be mended. The sinning brother or sister who now has repented strongly will desire to set things right (2 Cor. 7:10-11). This is normal Christianity. We know to look for "*fruit in keeping with repentance*" (Luke 3:8). Such a demonstration of repentance agrees with all that God says in the Bible, is recognizable as an intentional loving attitude toward others, and over time rebuilds trust. Your successful participation in such a divine enterprise will bring glory to the name of Jesus Christ, increase your faith, bring you joy, bless other Christians, and turn your initial courage into wisdom based on experience. Not bad for a day's work.

Three cautions are in order.

First, make certain you want the sinning Christian's relationship restored with God. Often we are tempted merely to want the sinning Christian's behavior to change. This can occur when the sinning Christian decides to sin more carefully. The issue is not whether we sin. Christians sin. The issue is whether the blood of Christ enables us to enjoy God's presence and holy influence. The issue is not whether the sins of others embarrass us. The issue is whether we will we glorify Jesus Christ by loving the lost and loving the "found" in a way that restores them to being filled with the Spirit. Consider this example: If I am caught in a sin, you might only influence me to be more sneaky and then to proclaim publicly that I have repented. You no longer are embarrassed by my sin and think the problem is solved. This is a lot like pinching the fuse on a bomb once and walking away because you are too impatient to make sure the fuse is out (Jas. 1:14-s15).

Second, be wary of thinking that the offense primarily is against you or the church. When I confront someone to "restore" that person and I have an inadequate idea of "to" what they are to be restored, then my cooperation with God in the process is unfocused and even incidental. The grace of God may bring success, but He is doing so without my direct and intentional cooperation. When God succeeds in restoring the sinning Christian to fellowship, I may not even realize it has occurred, because I am looking for restoration to a circumstance that is inadequate. I am embarrassed to try to restore a sinning Christian to fellowship and then have that person complete the work of God by restoring me to fellowship. At least being humiliated in such a way can make me humble. Our God has a sense of humor.

The third caution regards using guilt and threats in an unloving way. Everyone who is involved in church leadership eventually will need to confront a Christian who is sinning. Entering into the confrontation with a predetermined goal of "winning" the confrontation is easy. We all are tempted to consider the confrontation as a contest of opinions in which the "winner" publicly will be known. In such a twisted conflict, to use truth in a persuasive way is logical. Everything God has said is true. Guilt is real. God will oppose the proud. Unrepentant sin has public consequences to it. Guilt and the threat of consequences are real and persuasive. A moral high ground exists that even unbelievers recognize.

But in God's opinion the moral high ground is the Great Commandment. While guilt and threats of consequences are true, communicating them (if they must be communicated) in the love of God absolutely is necessary. Here is a very sharp tool indeed. When you can use guilt and threats from God patiently, kindly, in personal humility, to build trust in a way that protects the sinning Christian's dignity; then the person actually will end up grateful to you. You have just been blessed by God Himself as an example of a "pleasant somebody who gains much". Using the Bible to reveal guilt and the threats of consequences in an unloving manner makes you an example of an "annoying nobody who gains nothing". (Hmm! Isn't that a threat?).

Let's look again at the first part of Galatians 6:1.

Brothers, if someone is caught in a sin, you who are spiritual should restore him gently.

Is this evidence that the American church could improve from indirect, occasional, and incidental cooperation with the Great Commandment to a direct, constant, intentional focus on the love of God? A lot of people in your church are caught in a sin. Who is supposed to go to them? Those who are spiritual!

Those who are spiritual will go, and do go. Those who do not go are not spiritual. A certificate of ordination and a diploma do not help. Those who are spiritual go; they go often.

Faithfully going with an intentional focus on loving a sinning person will result (as the months turn into years) in skill and remarkable success. As the church remarks on your success, you will get more opportunity. Faithfulness to love people through years of opportunities makes you a mentor to those who look for examples of how to live and how to minister. Careful instruction from God's Word combined with the faithful example of the instructor results in a larger number of spiritual disciples who have a more holy influence throughout the congregation. You who are spiritual know this is true. You who want to be spiritual can choose to try. Have courage to try.

Or you could just let the devil (accuser, slanderer, liar) do what he wants in your church because you (though light) are afraid of the dark.

No biblical perspective on confrontation would be adequate without addressing the passage in Matthew about "church discipline".

> "*If your brother sins against you, go and show him his fault, just between the two of you. If he listens to you, you have won your brother over. But if he will not listen, take one or two others along, so that every matter may be established by the testimony of two or three witnesses. If he refuses to listen to them, tell it to the church; and if he refuses to listen even to the church, treat him as you would a pagan or a tax collector*" (Matt. 18:15-17).

God wants us to try and get along. When someone sins against you, God's will always is for you to talk with the person about it. Doing this in harmony with the Holy Spirit always is a good idea. The Counselor, the Guide, the Teacher who is the Holy Spirit is the key person involved in this confrontation. On purpose He will be loving. In light of the Great Commandment, obey this way: If someone sins against you, go and, on purpose, love that person and reveal his or her fault, just between the two of you.

When you go in patience, kindness, politeness, humility, and with your anger under submission to the unselfish love of God, then you are most likely to succeed. If you want to please God, then obey God's way. If your brother is open to the loving God who is Jesus Christ, then being like Christ is the best way to convince your brother.

Most people who are unwilling to follow this passage have a somewhat twisted idea about what should occur. Often, those who go have their lists of accusations foremost in mind. They are going to accuse and win a confrontation. They are going to talk and not to listen. They have make up their minds already and are unwilling to rethink the issues in a considerate and loving manner. If you have concluded that you are at war, do not be surprised if the other person concludes he or she is under attack.

When you have gone to your fellow Christian lovingly and have been rebuffed, take along one or two others. Take along one or two others who are skilled at loving people. Take along one or two others who realize that God has a "side" and that the issue is love and confrontation, not an assault with reinforcements. The person you are attempting to win will know the difference. If the person feels under attack, he or she will bar the gates.

Note that you are taking along one or two others so that every matter may be established by the testimony of witnesses. The matters to be established are more than just whether the person sinned against you or not. The matters to be established are whether or not the Great Commandment was followed.

If my fellow Christian sins against me and I go to him or her and sin by being an annoying nobody who gains nothing, then the testimony of the witnesses includes that I sinfully tried to win my fellow believer from sinning against me. The testimony of the witnesses includes the observation that the Christians both are sinning against each other. The loving nature of the witnesses ideally works to encourage both sinning persons to repent.

These often are the steps that enable Christians to be salt and light. These are the steps that often enable Christians to be like Jesus in this world. At times you will sin against another person and vice versa. This is inevitable; it's just a matter of time. If you conclude that you will not try to mature the relationship by doing what God commands, then you cripple whatever fellowship could have existed. You can't continue to cooperate with someone who sins against you. To refuse this exercise in maturity is to ensure short-term relationships and severe disappointment.

Remember that cooperation with the will of God is a matter of faith and not perfection. Give the will of God your best, honest attempt. When you sin, admit it, ask forgiveness, make amends for your sin in the ways in which you can, and try again. God is aware that you faithfully can try and fail. As He teaches you humility followed by renewed effort, He will reward you with extraordinary success.

If the sinning Christian does not listen to the loving individual and does not listen to one or two other loving persons, then take the matter to the church. Note that *every matter may be established by the testimony of two or three witnesses.*

Witnesses are those who have heard with their own ears and/or seen with their own eyes. People who listen to rumor and gossip are not witnesses. If they present themselves as witnesses, they are false witnesses. Another sin has been added to the mix.

Beware of listening to the testimony of a person who will not stand publicly for his or her own testimony. A witness proclaims a point of view. One who will not attach his or her own reputation to his or her own point of view is, at best, morally timid. The person's judgment of what happened is suspect. If people do not have the faith to stand publicly for what they saw and heard, they are untrustworthy witnesses. Their spiritual discernment is immature at best; their testimony emerges from the shadows. The matters they attempt to establish conflict with the point-of-view of God (John 3:20-21). This is the very nature of gossip. Do not let yourself, your family, or your church be manipulated by gossip that pretends to be testimony.

Again, *"every matter may be established by the testimony of two or three witnesses."* Note here that the "matter" is established among Christians by "testimony". Americans have a legal tradition that emphasizes evidence. In the church we want to treat everyone equally and see all of the evidence for ourselves. The biblical method places the establishment of each matter by "testimony". The character of the individuals is what counts! Who has a reputation for honesty? Who is like Jesus by being loving? Who has the proven character of humility by being willing to admit his or her own faults and call them sin? They are the ones that the church can deem believable. As a church in this situation, make decisions based on the testimony of members who are like Jesus. This may be un-American, but it is inherently Christian.

Unfortunately we often prefer the testimony of those who are rich, powerful, or intimidating. Just because God's method does not bring about a holy decision among members of a worldly congregation does not mean it is not the only method to be pursued in a faithful congregation. Do not ignore evidence but prefer godly testimony.

Let me take a moment and state the obvious. If you wait until you have a public conflict in your church to teach this doctrine, you have waited too long. Even the Word of God needs time to take root, mature, and bear fruit. Instructing your family and church on how to discern the love of God takes time. For your loving example to prove the effectiveness of the power of God to those who watch your life takes time. For you to, on purpose, practice loving others directly, intentionally, and consistently takes time. The love of God is a choice and a skill. Once you are rooted and established in love, you will get a magnificent return for your spiritual investment. This is an instance in which an ounce of prevention is worth a ton of cure.

When a personal conflict becomes public, the congregation will react according to the spiritual maturity and wisdom that its members already have. Nobody can exercise tomorrow's wisdom today. The Spirit of God will cooperate with the Christians who are faithful today. If the congregation is uninstructed about the absolute priority of the love of God in everything, then its members will react with a love that is incidental, occasional, and indirect, if at all. Do not expect the promises of Scripture to be fulfilled if the priorities of Scripture are ignored.

Finally, if the one who sins against you will not listen even to the church, then treat the person as you would a pagan or a tax collector. Perhaps used-car salespeople would have been included, if they existed at that time.

Don't let your prejudice cause you to miss the point. Tax collectors, pagans, and even used-car salespersons are to be loved. We are to love even our enemies. Being a born-again tax collector or used-car salesperson is even possible. (It's true!) Being a high muckety-muck religious official (denominational worker) while at the same time being a spirit-filled Christian is even possible!

The point of the passage is that the Christian who sinned against you does not listen to the Holy Spirit, even when the whole church lovingly confronts with the person's sin. Such people do not treat Jesus as Lord. They prefer their sins. They are lost or act as if they are lost. They need to repent and treat Jesus Christ as Lord. The Great Commandment means that to win them, you treat them lovingly. You never give up, but the church does not treat them as if they were Christians.

I urge you to believe the Scripture to the point of doing what the Scripture says. A disciple doesn't just agree with what the master says; the disciple does what the master says to do. Cooperate with those who are like Jesus. Follow those who do what the Creator says should be done. Encourage them; let them be your examples.

Chapter 13

The Love of God
and Group Confrontation

Conflicts arise when the will of God and the will of people differ. My experience is that I have both internal and external conflicts. Some of the external conflicts happen because of other people. Sometimes my internal conflicts boil over into the lives of other people. Conflict always is uncomfortable. While I always can make things worse, I have found that the love of God is the best way to make things better.

External conflict is inevitable unless you flee alone into the wilderness. Yet external conflict is the arena in which Christians are salt and light (Matt. 5:13-16). External conflict is the arena in which Christians *shine like stars in the universe* (Phil. 2:14-16a). Either you will improve situations of conflict, or you will make them worse. Should you refuse to love people during these times, we'd all be better off if you did flee to the wilderness. Please leave now. Take the Bible and this book with you. Return when you have hope.

The good news is that the Great Commandment is the great solution to conflict. As you mature in your awareness of how to love people with an intentional focus, you will find yourself in fewer personal conflicts with others. People who love others do not cause as many conflicts as do those who are unloving. People who habitually cause conflicts avoid conflicts with those who are skilled and experienced lovers of God and others. Such habitual fighters avoid such conflicts. They do so for two reasons.

First, the habitual fighter avoids the one who loves God's way because too few people treat the habitual fighter well. People who fight sinfully still value one who is patient, kind, polite, and humble. Sinful fighters tend to return evil for evil. They will get angry with those who are angry with them. They will gossip about those who gossip about them. They will call others names, exaggerate offenses, and drag up past faults—especially toward those who do the same things to them. Since the Christian who intentionally is focused on the Great Commandment intentionally avoids such sins, little cause exists for offense. Loving others with an intentional focus greatly pleases God.

When a man's ways are pleasing to the Lord, he makes even his enemies live at peace with him (Prov. 16:7).

The second reason habitual fighters avoid launching on those who are skilled and experienced lovers of God and others is that in the long run, habitual fighters lose. They enjoy landing the short thrusts of insults and vents of emotion, but in the long run they lose influence over their own family and friends who observe the nature of the conflict. Even in the secular realm, virtuous character usually wins over sarcasm from mean-spirited people.

Let me take a moment to clarify the issues. The love of God directed toward your enemies will not convince the majority to spare you from being burned at the stake, if that is their intent. If people are intently antichrist in nature and you are their target and are vulnerable to their will, then you will suffer. If someone strikes you on the cheek, turn the other cheek, but you do not have to lean into the next blow. Do not associate with violent drunkards. Do not willingly enter an environment populated with spiritual cannibals. Do not poke yourself in the eye with a sharp stick. For every saint that God supernaturally rescues from persecution, a thousand more are martyred. Pick your battles.

Regarding one-on-group confrontations, nothing results in a holy outcome more than does the on-purpose loving of others. Love never fails (1 Cor. 13:8a). Whatever the infinite God intends to accomplish in any given crowd of people will happen in harmony with the love of God. What you and I want in any conflict always will be less important to God than will what He wants. He is not uncertain regarding the most important thing. Even in conflict you either are an "annoying nobody who gains nothing" or a "pleasant somebody who gains much".

Let's take a look at a popular passage of Scripture that addresses the work of God in all things (even conflicts). Note the reference to love and God's purpose.

And we know that in all things God works for the good of those who love him, who have been called according to his purpose (Rom. 8:28).

Now this Scripture is just as true as it has ever been. And it still says what it always said. But do you see the added emphasis on love and purpose? God works for the good of those *who love him*. Not those who emote toward Him but to those who intentionally love Him as He defines *love*. Those who love Him have been called *according to his purpose*. The purpose of God is the Great Commandment. The purpose of God is more than the Great Commandment, but it never is less than the Great Commandment. Do not assume that God is working for your good in every circumstance when you are an annoying nobody who will gain nothing in His eyes. Remember that *God opposes the proud* (2 Pet. 5:5, Jas. 4:6). Love is not proud

(1 Cor. 13:4). Therefore if you or I are proud in a conflict, then God is opposing us. Sure, He is opposing us for our own good. But don't you want a better relationship with your Maker than that? Being opposed by the infinite God is not a pleasant experience to be purposely sought.

Let me twist the Romans 8:28 passage a bit and illustrate the absolute need for on-purpose loving in every situation. The Apostle Paul does not say,

> And we know that in all things God works for the good of those who are annoying nobodies who will gain nothing, who avoid and ignore their calling according to his purpose.

God will give you the spiritual eyes to see Him at work in all things sooner if you will choose to grow into His purpose with an intentional focus. When infants first are born, they don't focus on anything. After months and months of effort they learn to focus. In the years that follow they learn about the things or people on which they are focusing. For the rest of their lives they interact with the objects of their focus. We are not born, nor born again, to spend all our time on earth under a $5 plastic mobile that revolves over our crib. Focus, crawl, walk, and run; then run to the battle. This too, is the gospel truth—the good news.

Does war imagery and battle language bother you? I just don't know what God was thinking when He used it so often!

Maybe what bothers you is that people about whom you care get hurt all the time. You are powerless to stop it. Maybe what bothers you is that you keep getting verbally and socially beaten to a pulp; you have lost confidence. Perhaps you reluctantly have concluded that no conflict ever is beneficial, the result never is worth the cost. Conflict is interpersonal war.

How do you wage war? Do you ever wage war, or do you always surrender? What weapons do you use? What power do you have? Do you want mature confidence? Would you like to "win" once in a while? What does God say?

By the meekness and gentleness of Christ, I appeal to you—I, Paul, who am "timid" when face to face with you, but "bold" when away! I beg you that when I come I may not have to be as bold as I expect to be toward some people who think that we live by the standards of this world. For though we live in the world, we do not wage war as the world does. The weapons we fight with are not the weapons of the world. On the contrary, they have divine power to demolish strongholds. We demolish arguments and every pretension that sets itself up against the knowledge of God, and we take captive every thought to make it obedient to Christ (2 Cor. 10:1-5).

Let's look at this passage sentence by sentence.

By the meekness and gentleness of Christ, I appeal to you—I, Paul, who am "timid" when face to face with you, but "bold" when away! (2 Cor. 10:1).

Paul's detractors probably were claiming that Paul was afraid when in a personal or corporate conflict. Patience, kindness, politeness, and humility often are mistaken for weakness. But these virtues are in direct conformity with love as God defines it. When a Christian, on purpose, loves regardless of the volume or tactics of the opposition, the Christian still may suffer contempt from the opposition. When public confrontation occurs, the goal is to please God and to influence those who are filled with God's Spirit. If the majority of those present are not susceptible to the Holy Spirit's leading, then the majority will reject the loving messenger. The majority of the "perceptually challenged" will be convinced that you lost. On occasion this will happen. Count the cost and get used to it. God says that you won, because *love never fails*. Those who listen to the Spirit of God—those who are really the "called-out ones" (church)—know what was happening. This is a fine time to practice walking by faith, not by sight.

When the Great Commandment is given its proper place in the preaching and teaching ministry of a church, and the leadership displays an intentional focus on loving God's way, the congregation is prepared for the inevitable conflicts generated by this sinful world. My experience is that a church that is led to understand and practice the Great Commandment never will develop a significant faction who can influence the congregation in unloving ways. Unfortunately for the Corinthian church, the Apostle Paul was away a great deal of the time.

"I beg you that when I come I may not have to be as bold as I expect to be toward some people who think that we live by the standards of this world"
(2 Cor. 10:2).

Paul addresses the possible need to be very bold toward those who think the standards of the world are acceptable Christian practice. During those times when a church is not experiencing public division, the nature of God's love is to preach the Word kindly and patiently. Such a church knows that a significant amount of time is needed for the Word to sprout, mature, and bear fruit in the lives of the disciples. The loving teacher intentionally chooses to be patient and kind and carefully channels the passion he or she feels. In 1 and 2

Timothy and Titus this is born out plainly. This is not to say that the preacher cannot be animated in his delivery, but the the gospel message is not nurtured by sarcasm or condemnation.

The wise in heart are called discerning, and pleasant words promote instruction (Prov. 16:21).

Yet when a congregation becomes embroiled in public confrontation, then a more direct approach is needed. God says that (Love) *always protects* (1 Cor. 13:7a). When the sheep are in danger from the wolf, the shepherd publicly confronts the wolf. Do this lovingly, if you want the Holy Spirit involved. This is the boldness to which Paul refers. In the New Testament are many examples of unfaithful people being named publicly. We also see many publicly named persons who are examples of Christians who have left the faith or distorted the truth to draw away disciples after themselves.

The fact that detractors of faithful Christian leaders resort to the standards of this world in large, public meetings and small-scale conversations is predictable. These standards are not mysterious. They are gossip, slander, accusation, and insinuations designed to raise suspicion and to appeal to the listener's fears, pride, and ambition. If the Scripture ever is used, it is used unlovingly and generally out of context. The enemy gets a lot of mileage out of this. Remember and watch how this works in your circle of friends. This will happen in just a matter of time. Remember: this is a sinful planet.

For though we live in the world, we do not wage war as the world does (2 Cor. 10:3).

This is a very simple statement and suffers little amplification. Christian interpersonal warfare is different than is worldly interpersonal warfare. God's methods are holy—far removed from what seems natural in this world (Isa. 55:8-9).

The weapons we fight with are not the weapons of the world (2 Cor. 10:4a).

The weapons with which we fight are not the weapons of the world. Christians are not unarmed. We have everything we need for life and godliness, to participate in the divine nature (say, wouldn't that be handy in a personal confrontation?) and to escape the corruption in the world (2 Pet. 1:3-4). Not only can you escape the corruption of the world, but you can rescue the observers who are godly. Further, we are thoroughly equipped for every good work (2 Tim. 3:16-17). Certainly contending for the faith in private and personal confrontations is a good work.

On the contrary, they have divine power to demolish strongholds (2 Cor. 10:4b).

The weapons the Christian uses have divine power. You are not alone in a confrontation. God is there, also. No one is going to defeat Him. If you do not abandon His plan and become part of the problem, no one is going to defeat you. Whether the majority agrees with you does not determine the battle in God's eyes. The faithful observers are the treasure God seeks. Trying the faith of the faithful is part of God's plan. That which transpires before the eyes of the observers may take hours, days, or weeks to sink in and have its God-intended effect. Fortunately, we can rejoice in patience. Right?

Do your opponents have their votes massed? Are they past rethinking issues and ready to resort to political power? Is their hold on the organization strong? God cares about the remnant. God cares about the faithful. All the endowments and wealth of the organization are secondary concerns. If you have these priorities reversed, you are on your own. Without divine power, all is lost. The fact that we have a God, and that He does act in this world, surely is a good thing, because without Him, we surely would lose everything, every time.

We demolish arguments, and every pretension that sets itself up against the knowledge of God (2 Cor. 10:5a).

Arguments are lines of reason based on assumed facts. In this context, pretensions are arguments that are based on assumed facts that are contrary to the opinion of God. Those who believe the plain-sense meaning of Scripture are the ones who will survive. They are the victors.

Through patience a ruler can be persuaded, and a gentle tongue can break a bone (Prov. 25:15).

Every biblical example of conflict between the faithful and the unfaithful follows one general pattern. The faithful contend, "This is what God said, so this is what we should do." The unfaithful believe other moral preferences. Such a confrontation in the church requires a Christian who knows the Word of God, believes it, has practiced and become skillful in lovingly proclaiming the Word, and is not rattled by slander, accusation, anger, or peer pressure. The Christian is visibly to be like Jesus in this world. The Christian loves those who are unloving. This pleases God. This convinces the faithful to remain faithful. This influences the unfaithful to become faithful. This is how you cooperate with the divine power of God. Since love never fails, I recommend you become good at loving people in conflict. God demands it.

Please be aware that a time occurs when division is past healing. When reason gives way to freely vented emotion and the teacher loses leadership to the rabble-rouser, and when such a condition worsens over a significant period of time, you are in a revolution. The group, church, organization, or country is in a civil war. I have no answer to such a mass insanity. Such times occur, but they do not last long; the attrition rate is too high and the emotional fever cannot be maintained. During such times protect your family and those who have proven their faithfulness. If you must tend toward a "side" of the conflict, tend toward the lesser of evils. But to do so, do not sacrifice the priorities of God.

A good question at a time such as this is: "How is any of this my business?"

Keeping your nose out of other people's business always is prudent. Try to visualize the following passage.

> *Like one who seizes a dog by the ears is a passer-by who meddles in a quarrel not his own* (Prov. 26:17).

In any church are individuals who are more responsible for addressing public conflict than are others. Certainly pastors fall into this responsibility. Being patient enough to let the pastors and proven elders attempt the first solutions always is best. Mature Christians may be so patient and humble that they appear timid. If they have demonstrated courage and wisdom in the past, then trust them in the present. Do not let your passion result in impatience and make matters worse. Proven character reflects on the blessing of God. Proven character is an indication of whom the power and wisdom of God will flow through. This is another reason why pastors and deacons must meet character qualifications before they assume leadership roles.

Even in the midst of patience, kindness, and humility the servant of God can demolish arguments. All will know who Jesus' disciples are by their love (John 13:34-35). From God's point of view, the main issue in all public disagreements still is the Great Commandment. Those who are filled with God's Spirit will recognize this. Public arguments become very complicated very quickly. The love of God can be communicated effectively by being demonstrated. Posture, facial expressions, and the tone of voice all are valid ways to express and recognize the love of God. The child of God can communicate and influence the group, even when others are speaking against them. Just remember, only those who are aware of God's priority of the Great Commandment can see the holy difference.

Certainly knowledge of the Bible is important. Among God's people the Word of God carries authority. The Word itself is alive (Heb. 4:12). Those who truly care about the their Creator's will obey the Creator's Word. Certainly knowledge of the culture, context, statistics, and personalities are important.

But the spiritual warfare is not about debate or eloquence. The spiritual warfare is about real Christians recognizing the will of God through the people of God who are loving others. Demolishing ungodly arguments is accomplished through demonstrating the character of Jesus Christ publicly and not just by arguing "better" than your opponent.

And we take captive every thought to make it obedient to Christ (2 Cor. 10:5b).

How many thoughts go through your head in an argument? I begin thinking so fast that my mouth cannot keep up! This is not an advantage. I cannot give careful thought to my angry response. Recognizing that you cannot please God by filling the air with verbal venting is a very practical humility.

152

Concentrating on patience, politeness, unselfishness, and a self-control that does not allow careless words to proceed from your mouth is important. Take captive every thought. Control your own mind. Set free those words that are useful for building others up according to their needs, that it may benefit those who listen (Eph. 4:29).

This is a supernatural aspect of our faith. But it manifests itself through those who practice it often. It is a supernatural aspect of our faith in that God is most active through people who love other people intentionally. Those who have an intentional focus on doing what God says is most important receive an intentional blessing of being like Jesus in this world. This also is very, very good for those who are around them.

Who will rise to this call? We have a desperate need for Christians to own their own birthright and to glorify the name of Jesus Christ in a way that the devil will not imitate.

Ministry is service to others. The American church is recognizing the awareness that every Christian is to be a minister to others. We are to serve each other. No better way exists than, on purpose, to love people God's way.

Serve one another in love. The entire law is summed up in a single command: Love your neighbor as yourself. If you keep on biting and devouring each other, watch out or you will be destroyed by each other (Gal. 5:13b-15).

Enough about conflicts. When Christians work together toward the Great Commandment, something magnificent happens around them. It costs no money. It works in every tribe, language, and church-growth paradigm. It facilitates evangelism and missions. It reaches all age groups. It requires no degree. Something is phenomenal about a church that reaches Great Commandment critical mass.

Chapter 14

The Love of God
and the Church

And God placed all things under his feet and appointed him to be head over everything for the church, which is his body, the fullness of him who fills everything in every way (Eph. 1:22-23).

Jesus Christ is the head of the church. He is our King and Master. He decides what is right and wrong. He decides what is most important. He is the infinite God who thinks everything through all the time. His wisdom is perfect. He has no peers on this earth who can counsel Him. On every detail He is in perfect agreement with the Father and the Holy Spirit. He is building His church; nothing can prevail against His will and His timing (Matt. 16:18).

Our King has been generous toward us in giving us the gospel—the good news. He has given us the truth so we can be set free of the power of sin. When the church gathers, He manifests all the fullness of the New Covenant that can be known in this world. The church is *the fullness of him who fills everything in every way.* While we can enjoy the presence and fellowship of Jesus Christ on a mountain under the shade of a mighty tree, the fullness of the Master is expressed within the church, which is His body.

Jesus has given the church the Great Commandment. The perfectly wise, infinite God has given us a priority that intentionally must be taken to heart. The core values of a New

Testament church reserves the top priority to an intentional focus on loving God and others with all of the church's heart, all of the church's soul(s), all of the church's mind (thinking), and all of the church's strength. This is necessary for the individual believer; this is necessary for the body of believers.

How the church can obey the Great Commandment

Simply put, the leaders of the church live a loving example and clearly teach the loving priority. Over time the seed of the Word of God bears fruit in the hearts of those who are willing to worship the Creator the way the Creator says to worship. The Holy Spirit teaches, counsels, and guides those who will worship in spirit and in truth to live their lives according to the great priority of the Father, the Son, and the Spirit.

"Yet a time is coming and has now come when the true worshippers will worship the Father in spirit and truth, for they are the kind of worshippers the Father seeks. God is spirit, and his worshippers must worship in spirit and in truth" (John 4:23, 24).

Everything that the Bible says is true. Christians: read it all; teachers and preachers: instruct Christians to apply biblical truth to their lives and learn to live that way. Certainly the Holy Spirit will enhance the faith of all individual Christians and will endow cooperation in keeping with an emphasis on a churchwide commitment to the Great Commandment.

Preach on the Great Commandment. Preach and teach the passages that speak of the primacy and benefits of the love of God. As you address biblical narratives, point out how the response of the biblical characters was loving or unloving (sin). Show how the other doctrines of Scripture are fulfilled by the Great Commandment. Consider whether the whole of the law and the prophets really does hang on the Great Commandment (Matt. 22:37-40). Meditate on God's overall purpose and priority as it relates to the details of each small portion of Scripture. One extremely bright example of this is in the life of David, king of Israel. David was a man after God's own heart. He loved King Saul according to the New Testament definition of *love*. This happened many centuries before the New Testament was written and regardless of how Saul treated him.

Memorize the Great Commandment. Memorize 1 Corinthians 13:1-7. Hold up an intentional focus on living the Great Commandment. Encourage Christians to obey what God says about love with a similar emphasis that you already place on evangelism, missions, service, and stewardship.

When your church leaders meet to pray and discuss the status of the church's ministries, evaluate whether the ministry is loving toward others. Are you having problems in the midst of your building program or paradigm shift? Are those who are relating to each other in the midst of these changes loving each other? Are staff members struggling to get along with each other? Assess the status and growth of the loving skills needed to move a congregation from point "A" to point "B".

When the church looks for the presence and power of God in its midst, let the leaders remind the congregation to look for the divine presence and divine power of God which He expresses in empowering His people to love each other. Thank God for instances of perseverance, instances of humility, instances of unselfishness, and instances of kindness, especially when the Christian expresses such love toward those who are giving up or proud or selfish or mean. All of these behaviors are evidence that the living God is living through His people. All instances of a purposeful, loving act toward another or a purposeful loving response toward another are worthy testimonies of praise toward God.

When you pray, whether in a small group or a large group, ask God to enable you to love each other. Ask God for the ability to love, the wisdom to love well, the endurance to learn to love others skillfully. If you need patience or humility or control over your anger, then ask Him for it. Treat the love of God as important; then the congregation will treat it as important.

In your discipleship program include a primary emphasis on the Great Commandment. The same it true for your small-group plan, youth group, nursery, and janitorial staff. It is the Great Commandment. If any effort is expected to succeed with the blessing of God, it is worth doing God's way.

If any activity can be called "Christian", then such an activity must benefit from consideration of how, on purpose, to love God and others. This is the truth. Believe it; begin leading your church in on-purpose loving. The benefits of doing so are called *blessings*. They are real, they can become common, and they are the essence of eternal living.

An intentional focus and the church

Let's assume you agree wholeheartedly that a person who is skilled at loving others God's way is a pleasant somebody who gains much. Let's assume that such a person is like Jesus in this world. Let's assume God, by grace, provides this person with blessings that have nothing to do with who the person is but everything to do with Who God is and what He wants to do. Let's assume that God also showers this faithful Christian with the blessings of obedience that still are by grace but require cooperation on the part of the Christian in question.

Now, let's assume 50 such people are gathered in one place and are, as a church, committed to each other. What you have is phenomenal. What you have is a place in which God is magnified 50 times. You have 50 different outlets for the love of God, 50 cooperative images of God, 50 voices and testimonies to the reality of God, and these 50 are blessed with the most intense cooperation of their Creator because they intentionally focus on what He says is most important.

This is the sign and wonder of the reality of God that is not spiritually adulterous. This is the best possible environment for the seeker. This is the best possible environment for the new convert. This is the best possible environment for developing disciples. This is the best possible environment for conducting ministry, keeping the next generation in church, producing healthy marriages, bridging cultural preferences, and anything else you can think of. This is an environment that is more like heaven than anything else found on the face of the planet. On purpose, people can do this. This very, very rarely happens if the church has an indirect, occasional, and incidental approach to the love of God.

God's definition of *love* includes the fact that love is not self-seeking. Loving people attend church with the intentional focus of loving those who are there. They do not go to church with a nebulous goal of "encouraging others". They go with a specific goal to encourage others to be patient, kind, modest, humble, self-controlled, forgiving, and unselfish. They go to church "deeds first" instead of "mouth first". They go to give of themselves. They go with an absolute focus on cooperating with the head of the body, who is Jesus Christ. They demonstrate that they are disciples of Jesus Christ because they love each other (John 13:34-35).

Certainly they are not the only ones who attend. Throughout the week they have made quite an impression on people.

Because they love the gathering of the church more than they do any other human experience, they invite their friends. Others attend because God just leads them there; He knows where to send those He is calling. If they find a "service" that is culturally relevant, then fine. If they find a different cultural flavor than the kind to which they are accustomed, then the love of God still overpowers them. They receive the strongest possible urging to submit themselves to their Creator and to worship Jesus Christ as Lord and Savior. The presence or absence of drums and guitars really is a very minor issue in comparison with the great priority of God.

In such a fellowship the virtues of holiness are demonstrated clearly to be superior to the temporary pleasures of sin. The peaceful and forgiving presence of God becomes as attractive as it possibly can be in a sinful world. The sinner has no better place to be. No conceivable environment exists in which the truths of forgiveness and new life shine more brightly.

If the Great Commandment is emphasized according to God's will, then the integrity of the worshipers becomes apparent. This is divine relevance; this is what being with authentic Christians means. When decisions are to be reached, they are discussed lovingly. Those who continue to disagree over nonessential matters continue to emphasize the absolutely essential priority of loving each other anyway. An unloving persuasion toward a relative paradigm is not allowed to occur. The new paradigm eventually may be adopted but not at the sacrifice of patience, humility, unselfishness, and self-control.

The leadership of such a congregation is selected because of skill and proven experience with demonstrating wisdom and obedience regarding the Great Commandment. The awareness of God's great priority for the redeemed is so pervasive in the teaching, worship, and preaching of the church that unloving individuals find gaining significant influence virtually impossible to do. While members of the body may slide back into sin, the fellowship they are risking makes the awareness of what they can lose very clear. Forsaking the assembling of ourselves becomes difficult when such a gathering is the most valuable membership we know.

With the Great Commandment in mind, let's take a look at a very popular passage.

> But the fruit of the Spirit is love, joy, peace, patience, kindness, goodness, faithfulness, gentleness and self-control. Against such things there is no law
> (Gal. 5:22-23).

No law exists against an intentional focus on what God says is most important. We find no law against what God says is normal for His disciples. In fact we find a Great Commandment emphasizing what God says we should continually be doing.

From a corporate (whole-body) point of view consider the fruit of the Spirit. This passage was written to the whole church, not to each member individually. If I read this promise and apply it to myself as a personal blessing, I am missing the point.

When the church is gathered, the church as a whole fulfills this passage. The application of this passage is rightly applied to a faithful church as a whole. The promise of this passage is to you and for you, but it happens through the members of the body of Christ.

What does a loving church "look like"? The atmosphere of the fellowship is loving (no surprise that this is first!) The atmosphere—the experience—is joyful. When you are gathered among those who treat you better than does anyone else on the face of the earth, then you are susceptible to joy. This

160

loving environment that is the church is the place in which the Creator blesses you in extraordinary ways. He makes Himself known; He ministers to your needs more directly than at any other place. The church is the *fullness of him who fills everything in every way.* Predictably this is the fruit that the Holy Spirit makes available.

The atmosphere—the attitude of the church—is peaceful. Biblical peace is having a blessed relationship with God from God's point of view. Worldly peace is the absence (more clearly the unawareness) of human conflict. Biblical peace is dwelling in the presence of God and experiencing His acceptance. Sin is forgiven. Leaving sinful habits farther and farther behind is encouraging. If a little success is encouraging, then being with many successfully growing Christians is many times more encouraging. In a loving, joyful, and peaceful environment sinning is more difficult. Expressions of sin, including unloving words and deeds, stand out so clearly that the individual who commits such sins seldom needs a rebuke. The congregation is so in tune with the Holy Spirit that all consciences are fully awake and becoming stronger.

The atmosphere of such a congregation is patient. This differs from individual patience in that the members of the body wait for each other. Rather than the worldly desire to "be first", the fruit of the Spirit demonstrates corporate patience. When the whole group is patient, the participants clearly can see the difference between God's holy people and the world. In the world people quarrel and fight to get what they desire. In the loving church people seek consensus. This is not to say that no one continues to disagree with the body's conclusion, but it is to say that people respect the body's decision and will cooperate with it. The loving church also is not inclined to decide on the basis of a slim majority but is willing to wait for as many Christians as possible to arrive at the same conclusion.

The loving church is kind. When people from a vastly different social strata or completely different culture attend, they find acceptance. The glances from Christians are kind and engaging. The loving church genuinely is interested in new people. A loving church is more interested in evangelism than is an unloving church. This can be self-evident.

Goodness also can be interpreted as moral excellence. Even in a church that loves God and others indirectly, occasionally, and incidentally, members will display their best behavior when they gather to worship God. God's holy people are most holy in their behavior when they are gathered as the church. My experience certainly is not exhaustive, but church members rarely violate the law of God in full view of others. Yet the offense of the indirect focus on the love of God is that selfishness, pride, and factions can occur beneath the surface. Then the atmosphere of the church quenches the Spirit of God. The glances from the Christians toward visitors become less caring and occasionally even hostile. We do wear on our faces our corporate attitudes. An intentional focus on the love of God brings divine aid to our expressions.

Faithfulness is, perhaps, more than believing the plain-sense meaning of the Bible, but it certainly never is less. When the loving church is reaping the fullest benefits of the blessings of God by cooperating with an intentional, continual focus of the priorities of God, the truth of Scripture is proved publicly in the most obvious way that God currently will allow. When God's Word promises wisdom and I can see people expressing wisdom all around me, then I am more inclined to trust all the Scripture. When I see the teachers and preachers demonstrating the power of God by demonstrating faithfulness to do what God says, then I am more inclined to trust what they say. Obedience enhances instruction. In the long run faithful and careful instruction from a hypocrite gets poor results. Entertainment is a poor substitute. How about sincere instruction in an entertaining and loving manner? What a novel idea! But the loving ingredient is God's priority.

Gentleness in a congregation often relates to minor, yet necessary, corrections. For five seconds Mom turns her back on the toddler; the toddler is on the floor and two pews away. Someone wearing a lot of perfume is too close to someone who is allergic to the chemicals in perfume. A couple of children, full of joy, are unaware that the senior around whom they play does not see them and might fall and break a hip. This kind of thing always will happen. When a loving Christian attempts to set the problem right, then individual and corporate gentleness becomes apparent. Again look at the faces of the people involved. The mom can show annoyance and anger or gentleness and self-control. The people in the chairs around her also will show their attitudes. The gentleness of the body as a whole can have a lot to do with whether people want their children subjected to the company of the members of the church. Christians want their church to be a place in which their family members—even their children—are respected. We all want a place in which the congregation can be trusted to love our families and not hurt them.

We live in a nation where social bullies exert pressure on groups. We live in a nation in which the rebel is tolerated and avoided. Not in a loving church! The Christians in a loving church have a form of self-control that extends far beyond that attainable by an individual. In the loving church the individuals are one big, unified "we"! The priorities of the loving church are shared by the influencers who lead. Dividing them is far more difficult because they are loyal to the Great Commandment. People who sin by devaluing the Great Commandment have little influence over the loving church. They undermine their own influence with their own lack of love. The loving church as a whole controls itself in a loving way. The attractions of the blessings of God are corporately believed and lived. Loyalty is formed between the members as they return the love of God toward the sinful world.

The Apostle Paul's emphasis on the fruit of the Spirit is an attempt to get the church to focus on what it could and should be. The kingdom of God is not a matter of what you must not do (law of Moses) so much as it is about what one is to do (Great Commandment, Gal. 5:14). This all is possible. This all is attainable. This is normal. This is for everyone.

I thank God for the diversity of church-growth paradigms. I thank God for cultural preferences in music and dress. I thank God for business principles. I thank God for outreach budgets and advertising methods. All of them work better with an intentional focus on the love of God. New ideas sweep the Christian culture in America. Stay informed. Pick and choose to your heart's content. But eternal life is about worshiping Jesus Christ as Savior and Lord. You must be born again. Once born again, seek His kingdom and His righteousness so that all other things will be added to you.

And you don't have to spend a dime.

Jesus says,

"Come to me, all you who are weary and burdened, and I will give you rest. Take my yoke upon you and learn from me, for I am gentle and humble in heart, and you will find rest for your souls. For my yoke is easy and my burden is light" (Matt. 11:28-30).

Work shoulder-to-shoulder with Jesus. He has an intentional focus that will enable you really to cover some ground!

Chapter 15

The Love of God and Wisdom

I do not pretend to be a wise person. All I can do in regard to writing about wisdom is to "give it my best shot." You certainly are free to disagree or improve on what I say. When your disagreement with me becomes profound enough that you stop reading this book, then your problem with me is over.

Let me attempt a definition of *wisdom*.

Wisdom is the ability to perceive a context from God's point of view, discern what God's purposes are for the persons involved in said context, and to choose behavior that is in harmony with God's purposes.

Biblically, wisdom often is found in the context of knowledge and understanding. But wisdom chooses behavior that works toward the furthering of God's purposes in relation to the raw data of knowledge and the possibly inactive nature of understanding. Knowing and understanding what is going on is good; to do something about it is better.

Blessed is the man who finds wisdom, the man who gains understanding, for she is more profitable than silver and yields better returns than gold. She is more precious than rubies, nothing you desire can compare with her. Long life is in her right hand; in her left hand are riches and honor. Her ways are pleasant ways, and all her paths are peace. She is a tree of life to those who embrace her; those who lay hold of her will be blessed (Prov. 3:13-18).

This passage begins and ends with "blessing". The Infinite God is the one who distributes the blessings that the Christian desires. Certainly the blessings of wisdom not only are related to the sovereign grace of God but also to the nature of God to reward faithfulness. Here the first link between wisdom and the Great Commandment can be found.

Our blessings because of obedience not only relate to choosing what is right but also to discerning which right course is most important. To love God and others with all of our hearts, all of our souls, all of our minds, and all of our strength is most important. All of the law and the prophets hang on the Great Commandment. In my mind this includes the Book of Proverbs and wisdom itself.

God is the One who makes the distinction between wisdom and love. Like love and mercy, the two are very, very similar. Since the whole of Scripture accurately reflects God's mind as if He spoke the words Himself, both wisdom and the Great Commandment are complimentary and are not isolated from each other. Therefore, wisdom is more than love, but it never is less than love. In the same way love is more than wisdom, but it never is less than wisdom. The above passage points to the virtue of desiring wisdom above everything. The Old Covenant believer would do well to pay strict attention and comply.

The New Testament believer has a Great Commandment. The absolute purpose of God in the New Covenant is to provide new life through Christ and to enable the Christian disciple to experience and cooperate with this eternal life beginning at the moment of his or her new creation. New Testament wisdom is not different than Old Testament wisdom, but the wisdom of the New Covenant is superior to the wisdom of the Old Covenant. One can say that New Testament wisdom is better than is Old Testament wisdom.

If wisdom is the ability to perceive a context from God's point of view, discern what God's purposes are for the persons in said context, and to choose behavior that is in harmony with God's purposes, then knowing for certain that the love of God is absolutely necessary for every chosen behavior is quite an advantage. In this age of the church, God insists that every word, thought, and action be lived lovingly. He commands that we be pleasant somebodies who gain much instead of annoying nobodies who gain nothing (1 Cor. 13:1-3).

The Great Commandment is an unerring guide to choosing behavior that is in harmony with God's purposes. It is a most profound guide in knowing what God is doing in relation to the people involved in any given context. It also is useful for spotting those not in harmony with what God is doing, no matter how accurate their knowledge and understanding.

The love of God clearly is the primary focus of the disciple's life. Perhaps wisdom can be found in learning how to love others and therefore be in harmony with God's purposes in every context. This is a worthy goal for parents, teachers, preachers, and pastors. This is far more valuable than is mere money, mere humor, or mere emotional appeal. In the New Covenant wisdom is the way you, on purpose, love on others. One still can say that nothing you desire can compare with wisdom.

> *Get wisdom, get understanding; do not forget my words or swerve from them. Do not forsake wisdom, and she will protect you; love her, and she will watch over you. Wisdom is supreme; therefore get wisdom. Though it cost all you have, get understanding. Esteem her, and she will exalt you; embrace her, and she will honor you. She will set a garland of grace on your head and present you with a crown of splendor* (Prov. 4:5-9).

Wisdom is supreme; therefore get wisdom. How simple! How practical! Certainly wisdom will recognize the primary focus of the Great Commandment. Certainly the wise are more effective for the indwelling of the Holy Spirit. Certainly wisdom can be seen more clearly through the light of the New Testament Scriptures. Certainly the spiritual babe in Christ can begin living a wise life through a simple, intentional focus on what God says *love* is. Memorize 1 Cor. 13:1-7! Begin doing what it says. Confess your failures as sin and be forgiven and purified (1 John 1:9). After accepting Jesus Christ as Savior and Lord, one has no better way to proceed than intentionally focusing on what the Lord and Savior says is most important. A degree isn't even necessary.

The words of a man's mouth are deep waters, but the fountain of wisdom is a bubbling brook (Prov. 18:4).

How refreshing! I can begin now.

A wise man has great power, and a man of knowledge increases strength (Prov. 24:5).

How encouraging! I have a worthy goal.

And I pray that you, being rooted and established in love, may have power, together with all the saints, to grasp how wide and long and high and deep is the love of Christ, and to know this love that surpasses knowledge—that you may be filled to the measure of all the fullness of God (Eph. 3:17b-19).

How inexhaustible! I never will get bored.

Certainly wisdom must be related to discerning what is best. Certainly wisdom will enable the choice of pure and blameless behavior. Certainly Jesus Christ was wise and offers for us to be like Him in this world.

And this is my prayer: that your love may abound more and more in knowledge and depth of insight, so that you may be able to discern what is best and may be pure and blameless until the day of Christ, filled with the fruit of righteousness that comes through Jesus Christ—to the glory and praise of God (Phil. 1:9-11).

How absolutely Christian! This is worth an intentional focus with an intentional effort. This is a perspective on the New Covenant that is worth taking to the Master with the most profound humility. This is cause for surrendering your will to Jesus Christ again and anew. Put this book down and worship!

Welcome back. Let's look at a passage that brings great comfort, although we hate for an occasion to arise when we need this passage.

Consider it pure joy, my brothers, whenever you face trials of many kinds, because you know that the testing of your faith develops perseverance. Perseverance must finish its work so that you may be mature and complete, not lacking anything. If any of you lacks wisdom, he should ask God, who gives generously to all without finding fault, and it will be given to him (Jas. 1:2-5).

I cannot possibly know what trial of your faith you are undergoing, but I know that it will get better or worse depending on your perceiving God's purposes for you about His Great Commandment. If, during these very difficult times, you love God and others, things will go better for you. If, during these very difficult times, you sin toward God and others, things will go worse for you. You might prolong the difficulties. In the midst of these trials God is with you.

In the midst of these trials God always wants you to love others. In fact, in the midst of trials, our love has more supernatural effect on those who are around us. The supernatural love of God, empowered by His Spirit, is a proof of the truth of the New Covenant. The more like Jesus you are during these times, the more likely others will see Jesus in you. That means that those who worship Jesus more likely will be more sacrificial in helping you. No matter how long a solution takes, love God and others. You cannot possibly find something better to do.

God says, *Love never fails* (1 Cor. 13:8a). In context, does this mean that some of the spiritual gifts will cease, but love will not cease? Does it mean that when you are loving others God's way, you never will fail to accomplish God's sovereign will? I think it means both. Regarding wisdom, love is a component of discerning God's purposes and choosing a behavior that is in harmony with God's purposes.

God is going to do what God is going to do. He is the Infinite God who thinks everything through all the time. When He considers the context of the difficulties you have while you drive your car, He also considers the consequences of the single-celled animals the tires are killing. He considers the ramifications of the death of the insects on your windshield. The Infinite God undoubtedly has an infinite number of purposes in any context.

Did I fail to mention that the molecules and sub-atomic particles of the single-celled animals and bugs are worth keeping track of? Perhaps you thought John 21:25 was an exaggeration.

Love never fails. When you love God and others, you fulfill God's will. We cannot possibly know the totality of what God is doing around us. We cannot possibly know how our behaviors, even what we breathe, will affect the future. The Infinite God deals with the details. We are just supposed to do our part and hopefully deal with ourselves.

> *For we are God's workmanship, created in Christ Jesus to do good works, which God prepared in advance for us to do (*Eph. 2:10).

Our lives are not random happenstance. From our finite point of view we may perceive that time and chance play a part. On purpose God does this. His desire that we live by faith requires it. The very nature of being finite beings in a vast universe and an infinite spiritual realm require that we live by faith, because we cannot grasp the nature of everything at the same time. But from the divine point of view, God is in control. The plans of the Creator are vast beyond our ability to imagine, but He has given us a Great Commandment that enables us to accurately and faithfully participate in every context. This pleases Him. This is His design. This can be your primary focus. On purpose, choose it, for this is wisdom. The one who pursues this focus as for hidden treasure is wise.

Chapter 16

The Love of God and Friendship

A man of many companions may come to ruin, but there is a friend who sticks closer than a brother (Prov. 18:24).

We love our friends. We all have a deep sense of loss when we cannot identify someone close whom we would be willing to call our best friend. Even macho males can say they love their friends, if they can say they love anyone. Each person wants to count his or her spouse as a best friend. Something superior exists about friendship. We even can get into trouble with God because sometimes we prefer our friends to His fellowship.

Friends are people we like very, very much. We like their humor; we like their hobbies; we trust them with our secrets; we believe they will treat us better than anyone else we know. Often, we spend our "free time" with them. We go on vacation with them. We desperately hope our families like each other. We like their company. They have our loyalty. We generally will do as much, or more, for our friends as we will do for our own families. Friendships are deep relationships. Some people have no greater priority than friendship. In our culture this priority is becoming more common.

Some even define *love* in terms of friendship. They are infatuated when they are in the company of their friends. They prefer the company of their friends to any other human endeavor. Maintaining the friendship becomes a matter of self-

172

worth. If someone competes for the attention of your best friend, jealousy and even hatred become aroused.

Friendship is real. The Lord Jesus Christ has something to say about it.

A righteous man is cautious in friendship, but the way of the wicked leads them astray (Prov. 12:26).

Friendship is extremely valuable. Friendship is extremely persuasive. A friend can exert more influence on your life and decision-making than anyone else can. Since a friend knows you better than anyone else does, no wonder this person's advice is on-target with your moral values. The friend hears what you say, but the friend knows what you do. Our friends can predict what we prefer.

Perfume and incense bring joy to the heart, and the pleasantness of one's friend springs from his earnest counsel (Prov. 27:9).

Our friends will give us counsel that is sincere; that tends to justify and stabilize the existing relationship. We like them; they like us. We don't want to lose them, they don't want to lose us. A friend really does care more about you than other people do. In the time you have spent together, many times this person has proved this.

Friendship is very real. Of itself it neither is bad nor good. But friendship is extremely persuasive. Good friends will carry you through difficult times. Good friends know what they can trust about you. For years they have watched you and listened to you. They know your consistencies and your hypocrisies.

You also know theirs. Yet you all still like each other. You accept each other. The relationship is valuable, in part, because it is so rare. Yet friendship can damage your relationship with God.

> *Do not be misled: "Bad company corrupts good character"* (1 Cor. 15:33).

We all realize this. That is why we are so concerned with the friendships our children develop. We know that what our children's friends will do is quite likely to persuade our own children. On the one hand, *"He who walks with the wise will grow wise."* On the other hand, *"A companion of fools suffers harm."* Who we choose as friends has a major impact on our lives. Another example is:

> *Do not make friends with a hot-tempered man, do not associate with one easily angered, or you may learn his ways and get yourself ensnared* (Prov. 22:24-25).

To the person who cares what God wants (God calls such persons *Christians*), this raises two very important questions. Can I do anything to preserve some of my best friendships? And also: How can I choose godly people as friends that I really like? The love of God best answers both questions.

About the first question, evaluate your friendship. What do you do with your friend? Do you spend a lot of time sinning together? Is your shared affinity sinful? Are you friends in the sense that you enjoy each other's company around morally neutral settings, or are you partners in spiritual crime? Do you really like the person, or are you only fond of what being with the person brings to you? If the friendship is built around sinful activity, then bad company *is* corrupting your good morals. Of course, maybe your company is corrupting the character of your friend, but we will let that go.

174

The chances of preserving a friendship that is based on sin is minimal. But possibly it requires your repentance from acts that lead to death to an intentional focus on loving God and others. When Christians sin, their love is shrouded. The Holy Spirit does not empower the sinning Christian to love others when the sinning Christian is quenching the Holy Spirit. Isn't that obvious? However, when you repent and, on purpose, love, then the hypocrisies that your partner has been tolerating are gone.

Instead, your friend sees a very rare person who miraculously is changed. The person will be open to the reasons for your change. If the person cares for you enough to hang around for a couple of months, the friend may want what you now are living. You can be praying that God will call the friend to eternal life. If he or she gets saved, your friendship may grow to new and eternal depths. If your friend dumps you, the person was after what he or she could get from your sinful company. From the point of view of God, you are better off either way.

If your friendships with non-Christians are not based on the excitement of sin, then the friendship may continue for a long time—maybe for the duration of life on this planet. However, be careful. If you are not influencing the person toward virtue, then this person is influencing you toward vice. You have no middle ground. The dotted white line in the middle of the road only is on the road to destruction. Avoid being on the road to straddle the middle line. See 2 Corinthians 6:14-7:1.

With friends who are not Christians you have the opportunity to display the love of God. Your love can earn the respect needed for you to be persuasive. Your friend can see your patience, kindness, modesty, humility, politeness, unselfishness, and self-control no matter what trials you and your family endure. This person can see that you are more then mere human.

In all these instances one clearly can see that you care more for the company of your Creator than you do for the company of creatures. This is good for your friends and good for you. Remember that one who loves God and others is a pleasant somebody who gains much. Remember that the one who loves intentionally receives the blessings of God without stinting. You are at your best when the Spirit of God is guiding you and counseling you. That makes you more likable.

Jesus Christ is likable. When you are loving others in a purposeful and skillful manner, you are as much like Him as you can be. If your friends abandon you because you are like Jesus, then you have to let them go. You still can pray for them and, from time to time, try to renew the relationship, but when people avoid you because you are like Jesus and they don't like Him, then they actually are avoiding Jesus.

Think this through for a moment. Friendship always is conditional. Two people are not friends unless they both decide to be friends. You have to like them a lot; they have to like you a lot. If either person has a mind change, what can the other do? You can want to be someone's friend, but if the person does not want your friendship, then all you can do is keep trying to be a friend.

Very commonly repentant Christians will have friendships that change or even end. The holy change is more important than is the human loyalty. A lost person may not think so, but the Christian has to decide who he or she honors. Will you honor your infinitely wise eternal Creator or your short-time (60 years or so) friend? If you choose your worldly friend over your Creator, then you are proving that *bad company corrupts good character.* In God's eyes it truly is a very serious issue.

Anyone who chooses to be a friend of the world becomes an enemy of God (Jas. 4:4b).

While this is one of the most difficult truths for us to accept, still it is truth. Our friends have more influence over us than does anyone else. God is serious about repentance from sin. God is serious about living a holy life. If you are going to follow Jesus, you are going to have to leave something behind. This includes leaving those who will not follow Jesus. Remember that *love rejoices with the truth* (1 Cor. 13:6b). When the whole truth of God is realized, it is recognized as the phenomenal blessing that it is.

That makes the second question by far more pleasant. How can I find a friend who is like Jesus Christ? This is one of the few areas of life in which you do not have to start at the bottom and work your way up. Instead, God says you can start at the top.

"You are my friends if you do what I command" (John 15:14).

Well, okay. Friendship always is conditional, remember? If Jesus wasn't the infinite God, then this statement would be rather arrogant.

But He is the infinite God. Your Creator offers new life through your Savior, Jesus Christ. As He is your Lord, He offers friendship. A friend is one with whom you spend a lot of time, because you enjoy his or her company. A friend is someone with whom you spend your "free time" and someone with whom you go on vacation. A friend is your favorite person. A friend is one to whom you choose to be close. A friend also is one who has chosen to be close to you. A friend likes you. You are one of that person's favorite people. A friend wants to spend lots of time with you. A friend knows you best and offers heartfelt counsel and sacrificial help. Having God as your friend will put you in His company. Having God as a friend will introduce you to His other friends. This is a momentum-gathering phenomena that will last forever and get better every year, until no more years exist. Then everything will keep getting better. You don't even have to be jealous of others wanting to spend all of their time with Jesus, your best friend, because He happens to be infinite and can give everyone infinite attention all the time. He even has planned life this way. I'm telling you good news here.

Of course the condition is the big question. We have to do what He commands. If that means knowing and perfectly obeying every detail of the Law and the Prophets, then I may as well not even try until I get to heaven. If it involves knowing and perfectly obeying every detail of the Law and the Prophets, then we won't even be in heaven.

So what does being Jesus' friend involve? Let's look at the promise in its context.

> "*You are my friends if you do what I command. I no longer call you servants, because a servant does not know his master's business. Instead, I have called you friends, for everything I learned from my Father I have made known to you*" (John 15:14-15).

A little more Scripture brings a little more light. Funny how that always happens.

We have been told the Master's business. We have been enlisted into the family. We are fellow laborers with Jesus Christ. Remember the passage about "*take my yoke upon you*"? We are working shoulder-to-shoulder with the Creator. That yoke is light; that burden is not heavy.

Let's look a little farther back in the context of John.

"As the Father has loved me, so have I loved you. Now remain in my love. If you obey my commands, you will remain in my love, just as I have obeyed my Father's commands and remain in his love. I have told you this so that my joy may be in you and that your joy may be complete. My command is this: Love each other as I have loved you" (John 15:9-12).

Remember that the Great Commandment fulfills all the Law and the Prophets (Matt. 22:37-40). Remember that love does no harm to its neighbor; therefore love fulfills the law (Rom. 13:10). Remember that the Law is designed to kill, because it convicts of sin (Rom. 3:20). Remember that God is highly motivated to empower you to live a life of love. It is the Great Commandment. Love is the New Commandment, the Law of Christ, the most excellent way. After talking about obeying His Father's commands, He says "My command is this: Love each other as I have loved you". An intentional focus on the love of God is the way intentionally to focus on obeying Jesus Christ so that He and you become ever closer friends. And when you love Him and others, and others love Him and you, and He is infinitely loving everyone, you have a phenomenal group of friends that never, never will end.

Just a small change of subject; then we go back to the love of God and friendship. When you focus on obeying the first thing first, you will find great spiritual success. That is why I continually emphasize an intentional focus on the love of God. Part of this relationship involves the passionate priority that *Love rejoices with the truth* (1 Cor. 13:6). This also means that Christians who love with all their hearts, all their souls, all their minds, and all their strength will embrace the plain-sense meaning of Matthew 5:17-19. Love fulfills the law, it does not deny it. Love fulfills the law; love is more important than is the law. Love is even more important than is faith (1 Cor. 13:13). All of God's words are important, but God has designated true priorities among what is true.

"Great!" you say, "but I prefer a best friend with whom I actually can interact. Give me something I can recognize as friendship!"

When you look at the interaction of people in this world, do you look for God's activity? Are you looking for some angelic aura around an icon? Are you looking for signs and wonders? Are you looking for the miraculous? If you are looking for what He did in the past, you may not see what He is doing in the present. Do you see Christians loving those who are unloving? Jesus is right there! He is present! He is interacting with the world! Why not be content with what the infinitely wise, all-powerful Creator is doing all around you? Why not develop the discernment to perceive Him clearly? That is what He wants! That is what He will do with you if you will begin looking for His primary manifestation in this age. He is loving people. How clearly do you recognize love when you see it? This is the right track. Move at the speed of your faith. What else can I say?

Jesus Christ also considers your interactions with Christians to be equal to your interactions with Him (Matt. 25:40, 45; 1 John 4:19-21). Other Christians possess all of the attributes you possibly could want in a best friend, except they will not go and sin with you. Spirit-controlled Christians are the most pleasant people on the planet. They are like Jesus in this world. They focus on and rely on the love of God.

And so we know and rely on the love God has for us. God is love. Whoever lives in love lives in God, and

God in him. In this way, love is made complete among us so that we will have confidence on the day of judgment, because in this world we are like him (1 John 4:16-17).

In this world we are like Him! You can be like Him. An intentional focus on the Great Commandment is the straightest possible line between where you are now and where you want to go. *Confidence on the day of judgment?* That is pretty nice too.

God loves you. Through our Savior and Lord Jesus Christ, He has forgiven your sin. He gives us eternal life. God says that eternal life is knowing Him and Jesus Christ whom He has sent (John 17:3). Like Abraham (Jas. 2:23, 24) we can be God's friend. We are part of the royal family as children of God. We are the bride of Christ Himself. These are rather magnificent opportunities. This is a higher calling than a human possibly can imagine. This is the eternal spiritual will of God; that is more real than is the physical universe. This is worth our cooperation with all of our hearts, all of our souls, all of our minds, and all of our strength. An intentional focus on the most excellent way is the best way to play.

Let's address one more aspect of friendship. When you have Jesus for a friend and your discernment is growing and you have a Christian who is a "best friend", be careful to nurture the friendship with the Christian. If that person is a faithful Christian, he or she will nourish the relationship with you.

Better is open rebuke than hidden love. Wounds from a friend can be trusted, but an enemy multiplies kisses (Prov. 27:5-6).

You and your friend will be tempted to sin. Sometimes you

will sin. The conditional friendship of Jesus still requires that you choose truth before friendship. When your friend sins, and you side with your friend, you harm your friend and yourself. Sin kills relationships. Sin kills families. Sin kills churches. Sin kills the confidence of young Christians toward the integrity of the older Christians. When you side with your friend against the truth, others will notice.

In some congregations friends have been siding with friends for so long that the truth is a casualty. Factions have developed around friendships. This is not Christian at all. This is not a Christian fellowship.

> *But if we walk in the light, as he is in the light, we have fellowship with one another, and the blood of Jesus, his Son, purifies us from all sin* (1 John 1:7).

A "good-old-boy" network is not Christian fellowship. When your friends sin, be among the very first to restore them to harmony with the Holy Spirit (Gal. 6:1-2). If we do not do so, we are adding our sin on top of theirs. For Christians this really is not optional. We need each other. We help each other. Love rejoices with the truth. The truth is that we cannot publicly ignore our friend's sin.

Consider the nature of *fellowship*. During a significant period of time a group works together. Between times of work, group members play together. They have a common purpose. They develop common traditions. Within the group they have very close friends. They are loyal to each other. They sacrificially care about each other. The problem is that this all can be said of gang leaders who are in prison. This can be said about the Nazi regime during World War II.

Christian fellowship includes all of the above (except gangsterism and a Nazi regime), but the most important element of Christian fellowship is truth. We walk in the light as He is in the light. We all submit to the plain-sense meaning of the Word of God, even when our friends or ourselves are to be blamed. We don't pretend to be perfect in this world. We admit our sin and the sin of our friends and let the blood of Jesus Christ purify us from the sin.

Christian fellowship is more than work, play, purpose, and tradition. Christian fellowship begins with walking in the light. From time to time sin will show up, but the loving way to deal with sin is through admitting our sin and urging those who sin to repent. The fact that an indirect, occasional, and incidental focus on the love of God often turns ugly when a church addresses sin publicly is a very sad matter. It does not mean that publicly addressing sin is wrong. It does mean that an indirect, occasional, and incidental approach to loving others is inadequate. Recognizing and following the leadership of spiritually mature people is important. Spiritual infants will make a mess. Spiritual infants cleaning up the mess make it even more messy.

When a Christian is focused and skillful about the on-purpose loving of others, then leading your friends to repentance not only is possible, it becomes a beautiful experience. The on-purpose loving of your friend is holy. The on-purpose loving of other people is more excellent than are the spiritual gifts. The on-purpose loving of other people is the divine plan for our religious experience.

Chapter 17

The Love of God
and the Spiritual Gifts

Follow the way of love and eagerly desire spiritual gifts (1 Cor. 14:1a).

When we follow the way of God's love, we follow in the footsteps of Jesus Christ. God is love (1 John 4:8, 16). Jesus Christ is God (Rom. 9:5). The love of God is His great priority for Christians. Loving God and humankind fulfills the law. We know who His disciples are because they love each other. Following the way of love is most important.

All of the Scripture is true and most reliable. From God's point of view all of the truths of Scripture are loving. Yet God has made clear that some of His words are more important than are others. When we fail to realize this, we can become people who love indirectly, occasionally, and incidentally. As this occurs on occasion we are found to be unloving. These times of unloving words, thoughts, and actions result in a personal expression that accurately is described as being "annoying nobodies who gain nothing". The fact that an intentional focus on the Great Commandment will enable the Christian disciple to intentionally cooperate with His Creator is worth repeating.

Let's attempt to approach the teaching about spiritual gifts from the point of view of the Holy Spirit. He is the infinite God. The Holy Spirit is infinitely wise, infinitely powerful, always everywhere, and eternal. He totally is aware of the unity and priorities of the Father and the Son. He is part of always thinking everything through to the infinite detail all the time. The Holy Spirit also is the infinite God.

The power and majesty of the Holy Spirit is coequal with the Father and the Son. He is our Counselor, Teacher, and Guide. He loves us the way God wants us to be loved. Experiencing His love as patience, kindness, politeness, unselfishness, slowness to anger, willingness to forgive, and ability to build trust is wonderful. He does not treat us as puppets but as young children. Consider this: He allows us to grieve Him and even to quench His presence!

Do not put out the Spirit's fire; do not treat prophecies with contempt. Test everything. Hold on to the good (1 Thess. 5:19-21).

And do not grieve the Holy Spirit of God, with whom you were sealed for the day of redemption (Eph. 4:30).

What amazing thing is this that the infinite Holy Spirit of God allows Christians to "put out the Spirit's fire" and to "grieve" Him! I continually am astonished that God is so willing to let us think for ourselves. Truly, we are in this world to learn the difference between good and evil (Gen. 2:9ff). Often a person may fear an intentional surrender of his or her will to the Creator, as if God will reduce such a person to a puppet. This is not my experience at all. My testimony is that God gives me more freedom than I want.

Regarding spiritual gifts, God will let us magnify them over His Great Commandment. The predictable results are annoying. Sincerely seeking to express the spiritual gifts while at the same time quenching and grieving the Holy Spirit is possible. This is not an indicator of cooperation or Christian discipleship. Even sincere efforts to experience and please God are worthless in His sight if such efforts are not loving in God's point of view. If our love of God is indirect, occasional, and incidental, then our cooperation with God is indirect, occasional, and incidental. Fortunately our cooperation with God can become intentional.

Love is not self-seeking. Christians who intend to live in this world, as Jesus lived, will become better and better at living unselfishly. Let us examine the nature of Christian unselfishness in the letter to the Corinthians.

> *"Everything is permissible"—but not everything is beneficial. "Everything is permissible"—but not everything is constructive. Nobody should seek his own good, but the good of others* (1 Cor. 10:24).

In this context the "good of others" is presented as what is "beneficial" and "constructive" to others. As we seek to become intentional in our cooperation with God's loving Holy Spirit, remember to direct our words, thoughts, and actions at what is beneficial and constructive toward others. This is very un-American, but it is inherently Christian. God's will is that you eventually humble yourself and honestly and rationally consider "others better than yourselves" (Phil. 2:3-4, see also Phil. 2:20-21 and Rom. 15:1-3a).

This unselfish theme continues prominently in the letter to the Corinthians. To rightly consider the texts about the spiritual gifts, consider the context in which such instruction is found.

The apostle Paul continues,

> *—even as I try to please everybody in every way. For I am not seeking my own good but the good of many, so*

that they may be saved. Follow my example, as I follow the example of Christ (1 Cor. 10:33-11:1).

We are to follow the unselfish example of Jesus Christ. Some time read through the gospels and see if you can find a single instance in which Jesus did something purely for Himself. Jesus lived a totally unselfish life. He states repeatedly that He does only what the Father tells Him to do and only says what the Father tells Him to say. Jesus laid down His life for others every single day, not just on the day of His crucifixion. Everything Jesus did is consistent with an intentional focus on the Great Commandment. Everything Jesus did is consistent with an intentional focus on building up the people around Him. This is the same with the Holy Spirit in the church.

Now to each one the manifestation of the Spirit is given for the common good (1 Cor. 12:7).

The letter moves from addressing the way the church (body of Christ) observes the Lord's Supper to the body of Christ as a single unit, possessed by one Spirit. This teaching is in the context of the spiritual gifts that God gives to the church through the Holy Spirit. The Holy Spirit is manifesting (making known, revealing) Himself within the gathering of Christians. The "manifestation" of the Spirit is the direct intervention of God in the lives of the Christians. Such an occurrence is inherently supernatural. If such a supernatural manifestation is the work of the Holy Spirit of God, it also is inherently unselfish.

Now to each one the manifestation of the Spirit is given for the common good (1 Cor. 12:7).

The genuine expression of the Holy Spirit's gifts are recognized by the unselfish nature of the expression. The person expressing the manifestation of the Spirit is not the one who benefits from the expression. The manifestation of the Spirit is for the common good, not for the benefit of the one exhibiting the manifestation. The expression of the spiritual gift will be constructive and beneficial to those around the one who is expressing the gift. When we are filled by God's spirit and are in cooperation with Him, we will be unselfish in word and deed. We actually will glorify God instead of ourselves. We will live the unselfish public life that Jesus lived.

(Love) is not self-seeking (1 Cor. 13:5).

Since love is not self-seeking, the Holy Spirit actively reveals Himself only through unselfishness. The Holy Spirit has an intentional focus on the great priority of God. Remember that grieving and quenching the Holy Spirit is possible. While He allows us to be unloving in our religion, He does not empower us to sin. No matter how sincere we may be in our expression of spiritual gifting, believing that the Holy Spirit empowers "annoying nobodies who gain nothing" is absurd. While He allows Himself to be quenched and/or grieved, He does not allow Himself to be manipulated. While He allows His gifts to be misunderstood and misperceived, He does provide a simple way to discern what spirit is at work. The faithful disciple who lives for an intentional focus on the great priorities of God will have the wisdom to tell the difference. Again, follow after love; our desire for spiritual gifting is secondary. Love is the most excellent way (1 Cor. 12:31b).

Follow the way of love and eagerly desire spiritual gifts (1 Cor. 14:1a).

188

Eagerly desire spiritual gifts! Please do not interpret this chapter as admonishing you to ignore the spiritual gifts. This chapter is about becoming more potent in your expression of the spiritual gifts. The Holy Spirit empowers those who will love God (and people) with all their hearts, all their souls, all their minds, and all their strength. Such a description of our necessary commitment to the Great Commandment exceeds mere eagerness. On our pilgrimage through this life we follow the way of love. During the journey we eagerly desire the spiritual gifts. Journeying on the path of spiritual gifts and occasionally nodding in the direction of the Great Commandment is a sin. To do so is to miss the way. Remember that eternal life is more than just the first necessary step of securing rescue from the wrath of God. Eternal life is forever. Life on this planet only is a vapor that soon will dissipate. Eternal life is forever; the Great Commandment is God's eternal priority.

The manifestation of the Spirit of God through the spiritual gifts always will be loving in nature. Since such a manifestation is loving; it always will be unselfish and will bring strength, encouragement, and comfort to others.

But everyone who prophesies speaks to men for their strengthening, encouragement and comfort. He who speaks in a tongue edifies himself, but he who prophesies edifies the church (1 Cor. 14:3-4).

The word *edifies* means to "build up" and "encourage". When someone prophesies, that person tells others what God has said. God's Word then accomplishes God's intention. An intentional focus on lovingly proclaiming God's Word insures the closest cooperation with the empowering work of the Holy Spirit. This is unselfish and builds up the church.

In the context of the above passage, one who speaks in a tongue (real language) only builds up himself or herself, unless someone is there to interpret the real language so that the church can be encouraged together (1 Cor. 14:5). According to 1 Corinthians 14:4 you can edify yourself by speaking in a real language that no one else understands. However, in the larger context of the teaching about the unselfish nature of the manifestation of the Spirit, we can make a superior conclusion that "edifying yourself" actually is a mild rebuke.

> *Since you are eager to have spiritual gifts, try to excel in gifts that build up the church (1 Cor. 14:12).*

When a disciple of Jesus Christ goes to church (the gathering of the "called-out ones"), he or she goes to build others up. We attend church to encourage and strengthen others. The church experience is not about what we can "get" but about what we can "give". God reveals Himself continually to those who cooperate with Him. People who worship God with selfish motives predictably find little of value. God will empower you to love others. When you are ready to live as Jesus lived, you will find the reality of Christianity.

The manifestation of the Spirit through spiritual gifting is revealed through more avenues than just prophecy and speaking in languages. Let's look at what God says about them.

> *And in the church God has appointed first of all apostles, second prophets, third teachers, then workers of miracles, also those having gifts of healing, those able to help others, those with gifts of administration, and those speaking in different kinds of tongues. Are all apostles? Are all prophets? Are all teachers? Do all work miracles? Do all have gifts of healing? Do all*

speak in tongues? Do all interpret? But eagerly desire
the greater gifts (1 Cor. 12:28-31a).

Clearly from the context of the rhetorical questions regarding "Do all have this or that gift?", not everyone has every gift. Clearly some gifts are greater than are other gifts. God is the one Who determines who can practice what gift (1 Cor. 12:11). While we are directed eagerly to desire the greater gifts, we also conclude that God will determine which gift we receive. Our "eager desire" may or may not be rewarded with the gift we want. We cannot have them all.

Seeking the gift(s) through which God will empower us to edify others is true and right and worth our intense effort. However, do not miss this: A better way exists—a most excellent way that is for every Christian. Every single Christian! What follows the above passage is the most important sentence of them all.

And now I will show you the most excellent way
(1 Cor. 12:31b).

In chapter 13 you'll see God's definition of *divine love.* God's definition of love enables us to love Him (and people) with all our minds. God's definition of love enables us to evaluate our spirits and persons around us. God wants us to know and understand what the *divine love* is so that we, on purpose, can cooperate with Him. God wants us to abound more and more in knowledge and depth of insight about love, so that we may discern what is best, be pure and blameless, that we may be filled to the measure of all the fullness of God (Phil. 1:9-10; Eph. 3:17b-19). The divine love of God is the most excellent way.

The spiritual gifts represent a wonderful addition to the most excellent way, but they are not the first priority. Since the spiritual gifts actually are manifestations of the Holy Spirit, understand that the Holy Spirit knows what is most important. He allows Himself to be quenched and grieved, but He does not allow Himself to be deceived by poor motive. The sincerity of our eagerness for the greater spiritual gifts does not justify our ignorance about what is far more important. If unloving words, thoughts, and actions (1 Cor. 13:1-3) are judged by God to be the fruit of someone who is an annoying nobody who gains nothing, why should the Holy Spirit manifest His power through such an attitude? Should the Holy Spirit enable unloving people to become supernaturally annoying?

The real manifestations of supernatural power through the spiritual gifts are miraculous. For my part I am overjoyed that unloving people are not empowered to work miracles. I prefer to be a thousand miles away from such people. People who do not love others with the divine love are dangerous. Unloving people in the church hurt other people.

I eagerly will cooperate with any person with gifts of healing or administration if they are focused on healing and administrating in a loving manner. Such people will be patient, kind, content, modest, humble, polite, generous, self-controlled, forgiving, rejoicing in the truth, protecting others, building trust, and persevering. Their efforts never will fail in God's eyes.

On the other hand I will not cooperate with people who assert the Holy Spirit's manifestation through alleged gifts of teaching and helping others if these people do not have a primary focus on the love of God. Too often such people easily will be annoyed, mean, envious, boastful, proud, rude, self-seeking, easily angered, keeping records of wrongs, delighting in evil, hurtful, suspicious, cynical, ready to quit, and doomed.

If my indirect, occasional, and incidental manner of following God's priority results in actions that indirectly, occasionally, and incidentally cooperate with God, then I also likely am occasionally an annoying nobody who gains nothing. If I do not have an intentional focus on loving God and others, then I have an untrustworthy intention. If I conclude that I am unwise in the "Christianity" that I have been living, then, has the time to repent not arrived?

Humility is recognizing your own faults and limitations. Confession is admitting such sins to the Lord. If you choose humility and confession, the Creator will forgive your sin, purify you from unrighteousness, and in due time lift you up (1 John 1:9, 1 Pet. 5:5-7). This all is very, very good news.

God created us to live for a time in a selfish and sinful world. He reveals Himself and loves and befriends those who recognize that He became a person also in Jesus Christ. He gives us new life and a new spirit and the comfort of His indwelling Holy Spirit so that we can live self-controlled, upright, and godly lives in this present age (Titus 2:11-14). Please recognize that Christianity is far, far more than just "getting saved". Please consider a life filled with hope for every day and for the distant future. Please consider a relationship with your Creator that is more than just reminding Him how much He suffered for your sin. Press on to take hold of that for which Jesus Christ took hold of you (Phil. 3:12-16).

Do not conform any longer to the pattern of this world, but be transformed by the renewing of your mind. Then you will be able to test and approve what God's will is—his good, pleasing and perfect will (Rom. 12:2).

Learn about *love* as God defines it. Spend more time and effort thinking about how to apply love to human relationships. Become wise about the spiritual realm of purposeful love as a first and absolutely necessary priority. Memorize what divine love is. Evaluate your entire life by comparing it to the Great Commandment. Watch God manifest Himself through the eternally real qualities that comprise divine love.

From childhood you have learned to use your eyes, your hands, and your feet to affect the world around you. From spiritual childhood be diligent to learn how to use spiritual eyes, hands, and feet. The spiritual is eternal. The physical is temporary. The spiritual is the future of your life, your church, your family, and your marriage.

Chapter 18

The Love of God
and Marriage

What can I say about American marriage? Regarding marriage, our nation has "pushed the envelope" to shreds. A sadly humorous definition for *American marriage* is "any sincere, no-fault commitment of generally-sane mammals committed to an unspecified time-frame". We abhor pedophilia and admire 20-something women who attempt to look 14. From culture to culture the priorities of marriage vary greatly. Our national commitment to diversity will ensure the eventual adoption of polygamy.

Pollsters are so accurate in their predictions that many fear for our political system. People assert that West-Coast voters are not bothering to vote in national elections because the winner already is known. The threat to the system is real. The pollsters are quite accurate. These same pollsters also tell us that no current difference in the divorce rate exists between Evangelical Christians and average American citizens.

Because of the unhealthy state of Christian marriage, blaming the churches is becoming fashionable. I think this is a huge mistake. The problem is not that Bible-believing churches have changed their message. The problem is not that the Word of God no longer is relevant. The problem is not that the Holy Spirit is tired or weakened. The problem is that the culture has too much influence in the lives of Christians.

Our children are influenced by their friends, schools, movies, and television. When they arrive at marriageable age, they already have formed their basic beliefs about love and marriage. Our children have heard what we say at home and church about marriage. They also have watched what we have done as parents and churches about the epidemic of divorces. Teen-agers and young adults do not have the wisdom of many decades, but they are not stupid. Repeated actions that contradict repeated teaching are recognized as hypocrisy.

All disappointments spring from failed expectations. When young adults have a naïve Hollywood caricature as their model for marriage, they virtually are certain to be disappointed. Americans use the word *love* for so much that it can mean anything. When Christians have an indirect, occasional, and incidental commitment to loving each other God's way, the result can be divorce followed by prolonged doubt about the value of Christianity.

An intentional focus on the Great Commandment by parents and churches can have supernatural results in the marriages of the children and church families. While this book is not intended as a Christian guide to blessed marriages, this short chapter can make a massive difference in the marriages that "are" as well as the marriages that "are to be".

No matter how strident the protest from the Christian culture as a whole, the Bible does not clearly define the details of what marriage should be. This does not eliminate the Bible as the best source of truth about marriage, but it does emphasize what the Bible says about marriage and divorce. Books will be written about what Christian marriage is to be in a "post-Christian" America. This chapter only will address a few highlights.

The Bible does not say that marriage is based on love. You cannot find such a statement in Scripture, because it doesn't exist. Christian marriage is a public commitment between biblically qualified people of the opposite gender to live as husband and wife until one of them dies. This definition may seem quite analytical and dry, because it is. But it is also biblically sound. God is the third person involved in all Christian marriages; He is the One that makes them wonderful. I value nothing on earth so much as I do my wife. She is my best friend, best counselor, best helper, and only "lover". I know her better than I do anyone else on the planet and continually see her spiritual faithfulness and growth. On the day of judgment no one will cheer louder for her than I will. More joy and encouragement enter my life through my marriage than through any other way. God blesses my marriage. He is what makes it all worthwhile. The supernatural advantage is superior.

Yet in America, people still treat the concept of "love" as something you can fall "into" and even "out of". But the divine love of God is not a puddle, pool, or fountain. People fall into infatuation. Infatuation leads to a season of sacrificial best behavior. Infatuation always will evaporate, however. Then the sinful habits of your spouse become well-known.

Whether this American cultural phenomenon is fortunate or unfortunate is beside the point. "American-love"-based marriages vastly outnumber any other kind. "American-love"-based marriages are impossible to understand, because the American use of the word *love* has too many meanings. American marriages are random clumps of infatuation, romance, preference, friendship, emotion, and physical intimacy. A miracle on par with raising the dead would have to occur to make an American marriage into a Christian marriage. But we just so happen to serve a miraculous God. We have good news.

If your marriage is strong, this chapter will make it stronger. If your marriage is a burden, this chapter will make your load light and give you divine hope. If you are looking forward to marriage, this chapter will give you wisdom. If you are looking back at what once was a marriage, this chapter will give you closure.

Nothing is more important in a marriage than is a mutual intentional focus on the Great Commandment.

Husbands, love your wives just as Christ loved the church (Eph. 5:25).

"A new command I give you: Love one another. As I have loved you, so you must love one another. By this all men will know that you are my disciples, if you love one another" (John 13:34-35).

Dear woman, do not even consider marriage to a man who is not already a qualified disciple of Jesus Christ. Be aware; such a man will not even consider marriage to a woman who is not already a qualified disciple of Jesus Christ. The qualification as a disciple is defined as one who loves others with all of his or her heart, soul, mind, and strength. From the very simple foundation of this paragraph you both can thrive on the trials and blessings of your mortal future. I'm only writing these words; God is the One Who offers the guarantee.

If you are married to a spouse who is not a qualified disciple of Jesus Christ, then your goal is to attempt to reach normal. God changes people all of the time. You cannot directly change your spouse, but you can directly change yourself. Throw yourself on the mercy of God and ask for an intentional focus on the Great Commandment. Begin to love your spouse God's way. Whatever supernatural influence God is willing to use to lead your spouse to become godly will be helped by your loving influence. Whatever supernatural influence God is willing to use to lead your spouse to become godly will be disrupted by your unloving influence. Grieving and quenching the Holy Spirit of God when you most need His help is most unwise. Many people do, indeed, reach normal. An intentional focus on the love of God is the most excellent way.

While the Bible does not define marriage in the detail I would prefer, the Bible does define the responsibilities of husbands and wives. I certainly am not going to address all the facets of God's expectations—only the most important one, the Great Commandment.

> *Wives, submit to your husbands as to the Lord. For the husband is the head of the wife as Christ is the head of the church, his body, of which he is the Savior. Now as the church submits to Christ, so also wives should submit to their husbands in everything. Husbands, love your wives, just as Christ loved the church . . .* (Eph. 5:22-25a).

I live in one of the most politically liberal areas of the country and meet lots of people. As often happens to everyone, conversations turn to what each does for a living. I do not hesitate to say that I am a Southern Baptist minister serving as director of missions. I prefer lovingly to defend the name "Southern Baptist" rather than to avoid it. I rather have enjoyed the occasions when I could turn the conversation toward our denominational adoption of the "servant-leadership of the husband over the wife" stance. My line of reason is as follows:

The Bible teaches that God empowers the husband to superior leadership in the family. This is what God has decided. But the truth of the matter has been clouded by the sinfulness of false Christians. The truth is that God does empower the man to be the first to be patient, the first to be kind, the first to be content, the first to be humble, the first to be unselfish, and the first to build trust. The husband leads the wife in all spiritual things. He is to be the first to admit his sin and ask for forgiveness, the first to be considerate and unselfish. This is what God says. This is the essence of Christian marriage.

If the wife wants to compete with her husband by trying to be the first to be patient, the first to be kind, the first to be content, the first to be humble and unselfish and build trust, then that is fine. I don't think God has a problem with that. But He will empower the husband to lead the wife in spiritual things.

These are rather obvious conclusions that are reached when we apply the Great Commandment to marriage and to the roles of the husband and wife. The Holy Spirit will guide the male disciple to embrace this teaching. The Holy Spirit will guide the female disciple to embrace this teaching.

Rebelling against a husband who is like Jesus Christ in this world is very difficult. How do you stay angry and resentful against a humble man who is unselfish, kind, content, patient, and self-controlled? Only an ogre could do so.

Husbands, have you concluded your wife does not respect you and submit to you? Do you make such respect and submission extremely difficult because you tell her where the family is going, what will be watched on television, and how the income tax refund will be spent, and expect her to comply with your sexual fantasies? Do you think Christian leadership is making all the decisions about physical matters in an unloving way? Only an ogre could do so.

Women, do you really resent the idea of submitting to a husband if the husband is empowered by God to set the example of virtue in the marriage? You have my compassion if you married an unspiritual man, but you truly *are* married. Hollywood may have taught you to be infatuated with the "bad boys", but they all are spiritual ogres. The best way to see your man converted into a real (qualified) disciple of Jesus Christ is by returning his sin with the love of God.

Men and women, if you were Christians when you married non-Christians, then you were blinded by some polluted notions about love and marriage. Whether you intended to or not, you made a lifelong commitment in the eyes of God. If you were warned not to do so and did so anyway, you hardened your heart about the rest of your life. A relationship exists between your willingness to humble yourself before God and His willingness to forgive and answer your prayers and bless your attempts to make things Christian.

If I don't accept what God says about marriage, husbands, and wives, then I have to accept somebody's fantasy about marriage, husbands, and wives. If I pour years of effort into bringing my fantasy into being, only to be devastated by reality, then I am required to accept responsibility. When I find myself at the bottom of a very deep hole that I have dug, I can expect that years may be necessary to dig myself out, even with God's help. God rescues us from His wrath and bondage to sinful habits and not necessarily from the earthly consequences of our sin. The on-purpose loving of others always is the best way to reduce unpleasant consequences.

On this planet a Christian marriage is a common miracle. Yet millions of them exist. If you don't notice them, you may not have not known what to look for. To find them look for people who place more value on loving others than they do on worldly popularity. Look for people who are more concerned about their inner virtues than about their outer appearances. They will not put themselves forward, but when others put them forward, they will succeed. These are the examples for you to follow and after which you model your life. The ability to love others has nothing to do with wealth, credentials, ordination, appearance, education, experience, or intelligence. The ability to love others God's way is a spiritual blessing sent from the Creator. Every Christian can participate. It is our spiritual birthright.

Men, consider (1 Peter 3:7) what being created female and being commanded to submit to your husband as to Christ Himself is like. Arrogance in this matter is a very serious self-deception. In the eternal plan the Lord's gift of leadership to the man is very brief. Since you believe the Scripture, believe also that we are the church—the bride of Christ (2 Cor. 11:2, Rev. 19:7-8). Our eternal role with Christ is feminine. God has quite a sense of humor.

This is going to be a difficult paragraph. I have a good reason for including it. Divorce is sin. It does not "just happen". Divorce is premeditated. Weeks and months of sinful despair precede the decision to divorce your spouse. Holy reasons for divorce are rare and still involve major sin. While God forgives divorce, please understand that consequences from it occur. Divorce is a premeditated decision to harden your heart against the express will of your God for the rest of your life. As long as you live on the planet, the consequences will follow you. The God of peace will be with you at all times; but the consequences will be with you, too. Enjoy the presence of the God of peace without the consequences of divorce.

Here is the reason for the previous difficult paragraph. I love you and realize that I could be divorced in a few years; that what you have gone through can happen to anybody. Yet, a generation of children without yet having made lifelong mistakes follows us. These children matter, too! Let's not allow the next generation to repeat our failures because we do not want to risk hurting each other's feelings.

Dear pastors and teachers, take this to heart. I deeply regret that almost half of your adult congregation is comprised of divorced people. You did not ask for this problem. But when you accepted the role of pastor and teacher, you did, indeed, accept responsibility for proclaiming the truth of God. Supposing you would offer the children of the next generation to be sacrificed in the fire to the false god Molech is absurd. Yet something too similar for comfort is happening across our land right now. Despite the epidemic of divorce among Evangelical Christians, pastors and teachers are very reluctant to teach the truth of marriage and divorce publicly because they fear those who have been divorced. By default members of the next generation are refused the bold truth they require for holy marriages. The downward spiral will revolve once more. Please do not sacrifice on the altar of your fear the next generation's opportunity for holy matrimony.

The courage to proclaim the truth in love certainly is yours if you want it. Such a message must be patient, kind, humble, gentle, and self-controlled. Let such a lesson be taught with words that are full of the grace of divine love and seasoned only with salt. As you teach or preach the message, set a noticeable loving example by your tone, posture, and facial expressions. Communicate with the love of God; the truth of God will be received.

This is true for married couples as well: Communicate with the love of God; the truth of God will be received. This is good for your husband, this is good for your wife, this is the most excellent way for your children.

Chapter 19

The Love of God
and Parenting

God the Father, Jesus the Son, and the Holy Spirit are one; they are of one mind. In infinite detail the infinite God has thought through everything; He has done so forever. God is the author of truth; we are not surprised that the Great Commandment of the New Covenant is present in the Old Covenant as well. When Jesus was asked what the greatest commandment was, He quoted and expounded on Deuteronomy 6:5 and Leviticus 19:18.

Hear, O Israel: The Lord our God, the Lord is one. Love the Lord your God with all your heart and with all your soul and with all your strength. These commandments that I give you today are to be upon your hearts. Impress them on your children. Talk about them when you sit at home and when you walk along the road, when you lie down and when you get up. Tie them as symbols on your hands and bind them on your foreheads. Write them on the door-frames of your houses and on your gates (Deut. 6:4-9).

God Himself defines *the love of God*. The love of God is not an emotion; it is a choice and a Holy Spirit-motivated learned behavior. The love of God is His greatest priority; it is greater even than is faith (1 Cor. 13:13). The love of God is not a means to an end; the love of God is the "end" that has divine meaning. An intentional focus on obeying the Great Commandment is a choice. Disciples choose to do what God says is to be done.

Rearing children also requires an intentional focus. If all you add to an infant is food, clothing, and shelter, you will end up with an 18-year-old something. The neglected child will be shaped by influences of this world. If God does not intervene and save the child, you will end up with something wicked. Children do not rear themselves.

By God's design, parents have the most influential responsibility. By God's design we are to impress on our children the commands of God. In the New Covenant sense this certainly applies to the nature of the love of God and to His requirement that we love Him with all of our being.

If you received a high-school diploma, then you put 12 years of work into the effort. If you want your child to become a fully functioning Christian adult, then plan for 18 years of the same intense effort.

Children do not rear themselves. Parents do not instinctually know how to rear spiritual beings. If you follow only your instincts, you may end up with a mature animal, but it will be wicked. This is not good for you or for the child.

Learn how to be a loving parent God's way. Make this one of your greatest priorities with your spouse. Read the Scripture, pray continually; find some mentors, read some books, and do whatever is necessary to find motivation. Endure parenting trials in a loving way; as the months turn into years, see solid evidence of success.

Consider that modeling toward your children the love of God is most important. Your children will get bored; demonstrate contentment as you teach them to be content. Your children will be mean to others; be kind toward them as you teach them to be kind. Your children will be proud and make excuses for their sin; be humble and admit your sins to them as you teach them to be humble and admit their sins. Your children will brag about the grudge they hold against a neighbor; be modest and forgive them their sin as you teach them to be modest and forgive others.

Further, lecturing is not enough. Just giving true information, even if at the "appropriate age level", is not enough. Through information, observation, trial, and error we learn about the spiritual interactions that God calls love.

Adopt this simple rule of thumb: When your child needs your attention about something that needs correction, always treat this event as an opportunity for you, on purpose, to love the child. Your patient, kind, and unselfish demonstration of the love of God while you clean up the spilled milk is more important than is cleaning up the spilled milk. If your teen-ager has an auto accident, ask the teen-ager if he or she is okay, find out whether or not the teen was loving in the personal interactions after the accident, and then ask whether the car is totaled.

For the fathers to follow the same divine design is highly important. When Dad shows divine power by displaying mature skills of the on-purpose loving of others, then his sons and daughters naturally respect him and want to be like him. Our sons and daughters compare us to other adults. When we are like Jesus in this world and the vast majority of the rest of other people are not, our children see the difference. Make no mistake; God will see to it that the loving man of God is successful. The mature Christian is both the immovable object and the irresistible force. When God gives you an "inch" or a "foot", you occupy that opportunity and no one can stop you. If God wants you to stay there, nothing on the planet can move you. Love is patient; if you are faithful to measure your life by the years and decades, you will see that what I have written unmistakably is true. Learning patience takes time. Fortunately, you have forever. Yet I urge you to learn the skill now.

American dads often believe their roles are to teach their children to be tough, courageous, and diligent workers. In the Christian sense, these are fine goals. In the wicked sense, the children are taught to be mean-spirited, angry, grudge-holding, seekers-after-entitlements. Any animal will fight if it gets angry enough. Anyone can become aggressive in protecting his or her own territory. Rage is not courage. Christians are more concerned about the Lord's priorities than they are about their own rights.

Christian maturity is accompanied by the courage and wisdom to return evil with good. With Christian maturity springs the confidence from seeing the power of God at work many times in each week. With Christian maturity springs the awareness that *to live is Christ and to die is gain*. Courage leads to effort, which leads to success, which leads to courage. I prefer upward spirals to downward ones.

Here is another difficult paragraph warning. I was not everyone's target in school. I was not anywhere near the bottom of the pecking order. But the schools I attended were savage places. Let me go down the list again regarding what "love is not"; you compare these attitudes with the attitudes of American children as a whole. Love is not: easily annoyed, mean, envious, boastful, proud, rude, self-seeking, easily angered, keeping a record of wrongs, delighting in evil, hurtful, suspicious, cynical, a quitter. These behaviors were common in my school experiences of the late '50s through the '60s.

Eventually parents have to ask themselves whether they want to send their children into an environment in which they are subject to these behaviors at all, let alone for 30+ hours a week. In response to this I hear our culture say, "Of course, not every child is as bad as he or she could be. Of course every child misbehaves once in a while. Only about 15 percent of the children habitually get into trouble with staff. What can we do? The parents of most of these children don't care about the children as much as we do. Now remember, this is America; you cannot force your definition of misbehavior on anyone else"! Any similarities to the above "cultural quotations" are purely coincidental. Coincidentally, they are wonderful opportunities for qualified disciples to love the people of this world.

Just be sure you do not sacrifice your children so that you will not risk offense to their teachers. You decide where and how your children get an education. God gave them into your stewardship.

If you do not yet have children, think about these things in advance. If you want to be a competent adult, prepare for it. If your children are so young they are pre-rational, let the short time you have left motivate you to prepare actively. If you already have children who are school-aged; think fast.

Remember the passage at the beginning of this chapter. It said that we were to impress the Lord's commands on our children. To talk of them whether we are sitting or walking, staying or going. We are to write reminders of God's commands and post them where we travel often. Take parenting very seriously, the rewards will last longer than you will. The consequences of apathy can hasten how long you last.

Train a child in the way he should go, and when he is old he will not turn from it (Prov. 22:6).

I love absolute truth! This verse is part of the inerrant Scripture—the very Word of God. It's absolutely true. Of course, the rest of the Bible may modify what this verse seems to say. This is a great verse because it holds out a wonderful hope. But it also refers to significant parental responsibility.

Dear mothers and fathers: "training" is much, much more intensive than simple instruction. Every family member talks about his or her family's moral code. It may be as primitive as "Just leave me alone." It may be as rigid as Dad's rules and penalties written down and posted on the children's bedroom doors. No matter how simple or complex, a set of rules, even if memorized, is not the same thing as "training".

In 1973 I enlisted in the United States Army. Through reading and lecture soldiers learn a great many things. But "training" involves repeating the desired behavior hundreds of times. "Training" involves repeating the desired behavior regardless of the environment or annoying circumstances. "Training" is a very intensive effort and takes superior commitment and effort on the part of the one doing the "training".

I have met hundreds of parents who lovingly train their children. I have visited many Christian schools and Home-schools that train their children in the way they should go. I have visited hundreds of churches that teach the truth in their worship services, youth groups, and small groups. Very few of the churches train our children in these environments. Now I like churches and what they teach. I like the positive influence of Christian children on my children. I rejoice in finding adults that my children can trust, befriend, and emulate. Church is a holy place; people generally are on their best behavior when they are at church. But a church will not train your children for you. That is your job, not the job of the youth leader.

Train a child in the way he or she should go? Absolutely! But God meant what He said, not what you may prefer He said. Teach our children? Great stuff! But nothing can replace repeating hundreds and thousands of times in all environments and circumstances the behavior God desires. God wants your children to honor Mom and Dad. God wants Mom and Dad to be worthy of that honor.

Training up children may take a few hours a day or more. Let's say that I am making very solid progress in becoming a Proverbs 22:6 parent. But about the time my child is old enough to go over to a friend's house, I begin to realize that other people in this world seek to influence my child into repeating his or her own desired behavior. This may be Grandma, a friend my child's own age, or a teacher at school. The motivation of the one influencing my child may be totally innocent. Yet sometimes the person trains my child toward unacceptable behavior. If I allow my child to be trained in differing ways, then I forfeit the Proverbs 22:6 "guarantee".

This "contrary training" is rampant in America. Remember that I am stressing the spiritual qualities known as the love of God. I want to impress my children with an intentional focus on what God says is eternally most important. An in-law may disagree. This is another wonderful time to demonstrate your patience, kindness, politeness, and ability to build trust. This is another fine time to remember that your children may be watching as you vent on your mother-in-law about "her" need to control her temper. When you need to remind your father-in-law that he is not the parent of your children, remember that you lovingly must do so. In-laws spot hypocrisy quickly.

I remember my time in high school. As often as possible my group of friends repeated the behavior that the whole group desired.

Certainly you can see the nature of the problem. Other people can influence our children with "contrary training". On the one hand I want my children to be protected from the interpersonal sin in the world. On the other hand I want my children to be in the world but not of the world. God wants us to be the salt of the earth, not the salt in the shaker. Christians can overcome the world. How can we carefully plan the perfect upbringing? How can we insure that our children are not twisted from the Way? Without divine help, a pre-emptive strike to eliminate everyone from the face of the planet who disagrees with you seems to be the only workable plan.

Fortunately God has something much better. He will help. We are not alone; we have divine help. The Holy Spirit of God will give us the wisdom we need, when we need it. But we can do many things about this. Recognizing our dependence on the infinite God can be a daily practice. Memorizing and practicing what God says we should do is most important. Practicing what God says to do, regardless of our environment, produces habits that are called virtues. Loving God and others regardless of how annoying your circumstances appear to be can be a third.

We can behave every day the way Jesus behaved; this behavior is what God desires. Have you realized we are being "trained in the way we should go" by our heavenly Father?

This brings up the next point about Proverbs 22:6. God Himself is our Father; He is training us. Might I say He does His job perfectly? He has enough time; He can make all He needs. He goes everywhere I go; when I get there, He has been there forever. He knows what I think and plans all my days. He is perfectly informed, totally wise, and has infinite experience. And He has caused-allowed (you pick) my rebellion against Him anytime I wish. God is the perfect Father, but I am an imperfect son.

Training a child in the way he or she is to go does not turn that child into a puppet. It does not destroy the child's will. I hate this about a sinful world, but if someone wants to be wicked, then the person can be wicked. Blaming yourself or others for another's willful sin is not particularly wise. Leave that for the infinite God to judge on the last day.

The New Testament explains the training of children in a similar way.

Fathers, do not exasperate your children; instead, bring them up in the training and instruction of the Lord (Eph. 6:4).

This passage of Scripture addresses the father's responsibility of bringing up the children. While the responsibility is shared by the mother, God reminds fathers that they are the heads of their families. Regardless of what our American culture practices, the responsibility is on the father's shoulders.

This is not to say that children who are orphans or who are living without a responsible father are doomed. They are not. When sin abounds, grace also abounds (Rom. 5:20). A single mom is not abandoned. Through the presence of God she is not even alone. But God's ideal for rearing children is to have both a father and a mother. When one is absent, consequences occur. The remaining Christian parent has to work diligently. Complaining about being a lone parent does no good. Since extra diligence is needed intensely, intentionally focusing on what God says is most important also is needed intensely. As always, this brings us back to learning the meaning and skills of the on-purpose of loving God and others. When more grace is needed, put yourself in the path of all available grace by doing what God says. Grace flows as a gift; additional grace flows to obedience. Since it is free and wholesome, get all you can.

The Ephesians passage speaks of bringing up children in both "training" and "instruction". Here, again, is the relationship of "doing" and "knowing". Memorizing instruction without doing what is instructed actually is damaging. It causes self-deception. God says *Do not merely listen to the word, and so deceive yourselves. Do what it says* (Jas. 1:22).

Knowing what love is without the corresponding action of loving others will cause pride (1 Cor. 8:1b). God says love is better than is knowledge. He is very serious about His priorities and authority. When we acknowledge His reality and presence, He interacts with us. *God opposes the proud, but gives grace to the humble* (1 Pet. 5: 5b). I have enough difficulty in this world without the infinite God opposing me. He offers His children the blessing of the presence of a divine Father.

What a wonderful gift we enjoy when we are members of His family. We have the perfect Father, who has unlimited resources, infinite wisdom, and most certainly will make us into His own image. His motivation toward us always is love. His will for us is better than are three wishes or a magic lamp. While He works His will for us, we enjoy a freedom that is wholesome. We are amazed at His power and wisdom. We are secure in knowing that He is our Father and that no one can frustrate His plans. God the Father promises and delivers on His promise. He does not exasperate us; He gives us hope and courage.

If fathers and mothers do not bring up their children in the training and instruction of the Lord, then the children are exasperated. We become exasperated when we lose hope that a goal is achievable. When we are exasperated, we stop trying. When we are exasperated, we stop wanting a relationship with the one Who is presenting us with goals and expecting us to meet those goals. We grow aloof from those who present us with ideals that we don't think we can achieve. If we still admire the goals and the giver of the goals, we do so at a distance.

In 1993 I became a director of missions (DoM). One of the main requirements for the DoM was visionary leadership. As I worked toward that goal, I suddenly saw that my imagination could outpace my ability to achieve what I imagined. I have a reasonable imagination. When I apply it to opportunities and problems, I can become creative. The more time I spend considering a problem or opportunity, the more options I discover. This taught me a couple of things that I did not want to know.

First, I never have done "my best" at any time in my life. If I had spent another hour in prayer and thought, I could have improved my performance. If I had been more diligent in the previous months and years, I would have done a better job. At the time this caused me a great deal of anxiety. Now I have moved beyond the anxiety to a point of reference closer to that of my Creator. I no longer expect to do my best. I expect to try in a faithful manner. What is most important to me receives most of my time. What is less important to me receives less time. I learn as I go. I get better with age. I am open to whatever my heavenly Father brings my way; that just has to be enough. The result is peace with God and peace within. Being faithful toward what God says is most important has made me more effective than ever before. Why I am surprised? It actually works. Go figure.

Secondly, I stopped expecting/demanding that others do their best. I cannot live up to my own imagination; why should anyone else? Why is my imagination better than theirs is? Perhaps faithfulness is enough. Why not recognize who is most effective and just thank God for that person? Why place burdens on the shoulders of others that we cannot lift ourselves? I suggest that we intentionally focus on the goals and priorities that God has described and rely on His grace to achieve the results He intends. Perhaps this would result in peace, divine success, and thanks to God. It sounds pretty good when you think about it. Give it a shot. Give faithfulness a chance.

Think about all the people that you know. Who do you want to be blessed the most? Godly parents want their children to be most blessed. So give them a hope—an expectation—

that God will help them to achieve. Make this an intentional focus with which God Himself will cooperate. As a dad I recognize that my dreams for my children only are fantasies when these dreams are not God's "dreams" for my children. As I consider it, who said I have the right or even the ability to enact my dreams on my children? Am I attempting to rear my children to pursue the adventure to which God has predestined them? Or am I exasperating my children by giving them my advanced fantasies that cannot be reached?

The father lemming imparted to his children speed, endurance, leadership, and tenacity, so that no lemming would throw themselves off the cliff better than his own children would. How exasperating!

Parents, bring up your children in the training and instruction of the Lord so that they will be blessed and empowered toward the eternal goals for which God has taken hold of them. Blessing is better than exasperation. Let us all take hold of the eternal life to which we are called. Wisdom and wonder reside in maturity.

Chapter 20

The Love of God
and Spiritual Maturity

People often hear the expression, "Many begin well, but few end well." Might I suggest that those who begin with an intentional focus on the most important goal likely are to make the most rapid progress toward that goal? Those who maintain an intentional focus on God's primary goal are most likely to be encouraged and blessed regularly during the pursuit of that goal. One reasonably can conclude that those who begin with the best focus will receive the most divine encouragement during their lives and will fare very well during their latter years.

While God clearly is sovereign in determining our future (Eph. 2:10), perhaps He has placed on your heart an intentional focus on obeying the Great Commandment. Choosing to serve God shoulder-to-shoulder with our Lord Jesus Christ (Matt. 11:29-30) is your birthright. If you find an internal desire to love God and your neighbor God's way, the Holy Spirit is calling you, by the straightest route, toward spiritual maturity.

After we have been reborn by the will of God, we begin to experience eternal life. While we began our existence as finite beings, we begin to grow to be more like our Creator. We were intended to be the image of God. In the New Covenant sense we are the image of God in which dwells the Holy Spirit of God. For the next unimaginable and infinite number of "years" we will continue to worship the infinite Creator and continually become more like Him. Having begun as finite beings, we never will "arrive" and become infinite beings. God alone is infinite; we always will be finite. We never will be God, nor will we ever grow to the point at which we are even one percent of God. We just can't get there from here, but we always can be more than we were.

Since our Creator is infinite, He never will bore us nor deplete His ability to amaze us. He is most able to inspire us forever. He is most able to inspire wonder and worship in our thoughts. Thinking and learning are spiritual. Actions that cooperate with Him are virtues. The more we know and faithfully do, the more He teaches us and transforms us into the image of His Son. This is our reasonable act of service, our spiritual act of worship.

> *Do not conform any longer to the pattern of this world, but be transformed by the renewing of your mind. Then you will be able to test and approve what God's will is—his good, pleasing and perfect will (Rom. 12:2).*

Testing and approving the will of God in your own life is possible to do. True to His Word, you will find the will of God to be good, pleasing, and perfect. If you continue to renew your mind according to God's pattern, you will find that God's will for you always is good, pleasing, and perfect. As your life on earth passes into the "great beyond", you still will find that His will is good, pleasing, and perfect. On purpose, choose this. Choose to cooperate with the destiny that He has determined for you; it is eternally good, pleasing, and perfect. Intentionally focus on what God says is the most excellent way and dwell on earth in the best, most pleasing, and perfect way that is possible for you to attain and experience.

In the parable of the sower our Lord tells us that the seed is the Word of God and that the soil is the heart of the hearer.

Some seed falls on soil and sprouts but is choked by life's worries, riches, and pleasures. It does not mature. The problem is that the Word produces plants that have potential for bearing fruit, but no fruit can mature because the heart entertains and embraces the world's temptations toward worry, riches, and pleasures. The worries, riches, and pleasures of this world stand in poor contrast to the Master's good, pleasing, and perfect will. If you prefer worry, riches, and pleasure, then seeing that you even have begun well, let alone have any chance of ending well, is difficult. Spiritual maturity requires producing the fruit that the Creator desires. To produce the fruit that the Creator desires requires that you desire the fruit the Creator desires.

> *"The seed that fell among thorns stands for those who hear, but as they go on their way they are choked by life's worries, riches and pleasures, and they do not mature. But the seed on good soil stands for those with a noble and good heart, who hear the word, retain it, and by persevering produce a crop"* (Luke 8:14-15).

A direct relationship exists between maturity and bearing fruit, or producing a crop. While saying that whatever actions your faith produces may be God's will for you is fair, concluding that whatever you do that is best in God's eyes will result in the best fruit in His eyes is reasonable. Direct cooperation is better than indirect, occasional, and incidental cooperation.

I dare say that any fruit you bear that is indirect, occasional, and incidental is useful in God's kingdom only because it is indirectly, incidentally, and occasionally an expression of the love of God. Being rooted and established over a significant period of time in the love of God is the prerequisite to spiritual maturity.

And I pray that you, being rooted and established in love, may have power, together with all the saints, to grasp how wide and deep is the love of Christ, and to know this love that surpasses knowledge—that you may be filled to the measure of all the fullness of God (Eph. 3:17b-19).

Note again that the love of God actually surpasses knowledge. We begin our pilgrimage toward intentional maturity by knowing how God defines *love* and in a loving manner choosing our words and actions. When we fail to do so, we confess it as sin; He purifies us of such unrighteousness (1 John 1:9). Then we learn from our failure and try again. As the months turn into years, we become wiser at understanding what love is and more skillful at on-purpose loving so that others can be encouraged. During these times of very spiritual experience, we observe that the results are greater than is the sum of the ingredients. In all of our efforts to love God and others, He is at work to an infinite degree and depth. We do not love God and others alone. God is at work through us. God is drawing us into His infinite purposes. His infinite purposes far surpass our ability to understand all that is occurring. The love of Christ is knowable in our finite perception but accomplishes the infinite will of God from the divine perspective. The divine perspective is yours to explore forever but still surpasses knowledge that we can attain.

While the word *maturity* does not appear in this passage, I think we rationally can conclude that maturity and being "filled to the measure of all the fullness of God" are deeply related. In the process of spiritual maturity we must be "rooted and established in love". An intentional focus on doing everything God's way is the quickest way to become rooted and established. Indirectly, occasionally, and incidentally we can become rooted and established, but the time required is much greater. This longer span of time includes many more temptations to become sidetracked and many more consequences to be endured. We often bring unnecessary hardship on ourselves because we attempted to live around others in a less loving manner.

Success at intentional love begins with a desire to do so. Fan this desire into flame. Throw yourself on the mercy of your Creator and plead with Him for the ability to love Him and others His way. Apart from Him we can do nothing. Daily remind yourself to seek His will. As you pray without ceasing, pray for the blessings of obedience.

Success at intentional love continues with memorizing God's definition of *love* in 1 Corinthians 13:4-7. Remember it and meditate on it every day of your life. Evaluate and interpret the interactions of the people around you according to God's definition of *love*.

Success at intentional love continues with prayer for the ability to love others. Ask, seek, and knock for patience, humility, and unselfishness. Recognize your weaknesses; ask for God's strength. Pray for the ability to love those you are likely to meet today. Pray on the spur of the moment for those who happened into your life unexpectedly and even for those who ambush you.

Success at intentional love continues with your purposeful effort to speak and act lovingly. Measure your success as a person by how well you bring kindness, contentment, modesty, politeness, and self-control into everyone's life. As you contribute your work to the world, remember that how you work is more important than what you produce. The love of God is most real. You may give it away as freely as you wish.

Success at intentional love continues as your heavenly Father entrusts you with more and more opportunities to love more and more people. Soon He will entrust very difficult people into your care. As you learn to love in all circumstances, you will be successful in relating to difficult people, regardless of whether they change. Changing lives is God's work, not ours. Loving people is God's work and ours. Our part is to love others. God determines the results. As you demonstrate faithfulness, God will entrust you with groups of difficult people. You still can be successful.

Success at intentional love continues without lessening in intensity or adventure. The love of God surpasses knowledge. Love is greater than is faith or hope. God is love.

Know for certain that God is highly motivated to enable you to obey the Great Commandment. Know for certain that the blessings of God will flow toward you and yours when you are faithful to what He says is the most excellent way. The love of God always is the will of God.

You have many other practical ways to improve your discernment and skill toward loving others. As you practice these, you easily will note your own growth.

At the end of a day, meeting, or personal altercation, do a prayer review of your faithfulness. If you desire, pray for God to change the circumstances and the other people, but know that the answer becomes "yes", "no", or "not yet". When you ask God to reveal your own behavior, you most certainly will get an answer. Run your part of the day's relationships by God in the context of, "Lord, please show me where I was unloving and how I can become more loving." When you do this, your conscience will become strong, the confession of your sin will be forgiven, and your character will be purified. Your ability to build trust will increase. As you demonstrate trustworthiness to God, He will entrust you with wisdom and opportunity.

Another part of a daily (hourly) prayer review is supplication. After you have removed the beams and specks from your own eye, you can see the needs of the other people around you. Beseech God to save them from sin by giving them repentance, on purpose, to love God and others. When you note a repetitive sin in a brother or sister, deduce the facet of love that the individual needs. Then daily (hourly) begin asking God to bless the person with the needed virtue. God's heart always is inclined to answer "yes" to such a request, though His timing and manner may seem mysterious.

Another valuable method to improve your skill at loving others is to find a friend (ideally, your spouse) who with you will pursue the Great Commandment. We all have a difficulty seeing ourselves as others see us. A friend knows you well. If the friend also is intentionally focused on the love of God, then that friend lovingly can point out your successes and your sins. The person even can do so lovingly, which stings a lot less. Evaluate yourself and grow. Evaluate your friends in a relationship designed for growth so they can grow. In the light of the love of God, with your friend evaluate movies and books.

Mentoring is a buzzword that refers to helping another to mature in knowledge and skills. In a Christian context this time is well-spent as you, on purpose, encourage your disciple to become loving. Both of you can help each other with insight about the behavior of the other. The tasks you assign to your disciple will be more successful when the disciple, with a loving focus, attempts the task. The mistakes the disciple makes will be less disruptive to the congregation as the disciple places a higher priority on the Great Commandment than on the common tasks of ministry.

Spiritual maturity enables the Christian to become influential in the public setting. Experience and knowledge always are important in helping a group to arrive at a decision. A timely word always is precious. Note also that a timely expression of love can be most beneficial. At times the demonstration of humility and self-control will tip the group toward virtuous behavior; nothing else will. Spiritual maturity will enable you to recognize the "teachable moment" and will empower you to inspire the best in people. This glorifies God and Jesus Christ our Lord.

And this is my prayer: that your love may abound more and more in knowledge and depth of insight, so that you may be able to discern what is best and be pure and blameless until the day of Christ, filled with the fruit of righteousness that comes through Jesus Christ- to the glory and praise of God (Phil. 1:9-11).

I have one more thing to say. Please give this book to someone who wants to be like Jesus. If you are going to read it again, then do so soon. If you are going to wait for a couple of months, then send this book on its way. For Jesus' glory, for the blessing of others, for the healing of churches and families and marriages, send this book on its way.

Order more copies of

The MOST EXCELLENT Way

Call toll free: 1-800-747-0738
Visit: *www.hannibalbooks.com*
Email: *hannibalbooks@earthlink.net*
FAX: 1-888-252-3022
Mail copy of form below to:
Hannibal Books
P.O. Box 461592
Garland, Texas 75046

Number of copies desired _____
Multiply number of copies by $14.95 _____

Please add $3 for postage and handling for first book and add
50 cents for each additional book in the order.

Shipping and handling$_____
Texas residents add 8.25% sales tax $_____

Total order $_____

Mark method of payment:
check enclosed _____
Credit card# _____
exp. date_____ (Visa, MasterCard, Discover, American Express accepted)

Name _____

Address _____

City State, Zip _____

Phone _____ FAX _____

Email _____